"WHY IS JESUS THE ONLY WAY TO GOD, THE FATHER?"

REVEREND LYNN AHRENS

Unless otherwise indicated, Bible quotations are taken from the *NEW AMERICAN STANDARD BIBLE* (1995 Updated Edition), Copyright © 1960, 1962, 1963, 1968, 1971, 1972, 1973, 1975, 1977, 1995 by The Lockman Foundation, Used by permission, "(www.Lockman.org), and the *NEW AMERICAN STANDARD BIBLE* (1977 Updated Edition), Copyright © 1960, 1962, 1963, 1968, 1971, 1972, 1973, 1975, 1977 by The Lockman Foundation. Used by permission. "(www.Lockman.org)".

The Lockman Foundation
1960, 1962, 1963, 1968, 1971, 1972, 1973, 1975, 1977
A Corporation Not for Profit

The choice to use the NASB rather than the KJV was due to this author's opinion that our culture has become unfamiliar with the Elizabethan language, to the extent that it is considered difficult or cumbersome to read, much less understand, especially for those new to Christendom.

Please note the author has chosen to capitalize certain pronouns in Scripture that refer to the Father, Son, and Holy Spirit, which may differ from some Bible publishers' styles.

Also, note that the name satan is not capitalized. The author chooses not to acknowledge him, even to the point of violating grammatical rules relating to proper nouns.

Finally, this author chooses to capitalize any pronouns referring to the Trinity, even to the point of violating grammatical rules relating to pronouns.

www.xulonpress.com

DEDICATION

As I began to write down thoughts about "Why Jesus is the Only Way to God the Father," I realized how much inspiration I had gotten from a very gentle and loving Pastor, under whose ministry I sat for ten years. This dear man took me under his wings and encouraged me to study and be trained in the things of God. Therefore, I would like to dedicate this book to Pastor Malcolm Brown, who never stopped believing in my ability to teach God's Word. Though he may not realize it, it is due to his guidance that I received my biggest thrust of spiritual growth.

I would like to also dedicate this book to my husband, John, who has been my co-worker in the ministry for many years.

Lastly, I dedicate this book to all of our children, grand-children, and great-grandchildren. I love you all so very much. May you glean and grow spiritually from the readings of "Why Jesus is the only way to God the Father!"

ACKNOWLEDGMENTS

Firstly, I would like to acknowledge the Lord Jesus Christ, who has been there for me, holding me up and encouraging me at times when it seemed that my world would crumble around me. He has been my dearest and best friend from the onset of our relationship which began in 1968, when I was introduced to Him by my dear friend, Sharon Pelc. To you Sharon, I will be forever grateful!

Thank you to my husband John, and to sister, Dorothy Van Dusen, who would allow me to work quietly on my laptop instead of interacting with them. I do so appreciate their understanding.

How can I express adequate thanks to those who helped me with the editing of this book? Maria Mellberg, Colleen Curry, and to my husband, John, you have no idea how much it has meant to me for them to take the time to peruse these pages in order for it to be without typos and also be grammatically correct. I thank you all from the bottom of my heart.

Thank you Pastors Weldon and Kathy Townsend, for your encouragement and for prodding me to not only get this message out, but also in having me actually work at getting this book published. Thank you for believing in me.

Thank you to my beloved friends and saints of God at Shield of Faith Ministries in Saginaw, Michigan for believing in me and encouraging me to teach and preach.

Thank you to my dear cell group girl friends: Tavy, Stephanie, Lisa, Janet, Jana, Brandy, and Susie, who have cheered me on in this quest to publish my first book.

Thank you to Tavy and Thomas Pasieka for all the help they have given regarding the legalities and procedural steps I needed to take in order to accomplish this feat. I especially thank you, Tavy, for introducing me to Xulon Press.

Perhaps the best help to me has been from my children: Sherye, Lori, John, and Tim, who would individually either make comments or ask questions that helped me to understand that certain subjects required deeper clarification and understanding. As a result, it forced me to dig deeper into God's Word, seek out, and use Biblical references in areas where I might not have felt it otherwise necessary. I love you and thank you for your contribution, even when you didn't know you had made any.

Jesus said,

"Do not let your heart be troubled; believe in God,
believe also in Me.
In My Father's house are many dwelling places;
if it were not so, I would have told you; for I go to
prepare a place for you.
If I go and prepare a place for you, I will come
again and receive you to Myself, that where I am,
there you may be also.
And you know the way where I am going.
Thomas said to Him, 'Lord, we do not know where
You are going, how do we know the way?'

"Jesus said to him, 'I am the way, and the truth, and the life; no one comes to the Father but through Me.'"
John 14:1-6 [NASB]

"The thief comes only to steal, kill, and destroy; I have come that they may have life, and have it to the full."
John 10:10 [NASB}

"I am the vine, you are the branches. He who abides in Me, and I in him, bears much fruit; for without Me you can do nothing."
John 15:5 [NKJ]

TABLE OF CONTENTS

— PROLOGUE —

Have you ever wondered how to adequately share why the Bible states that the only sure way to the Father is through Jesus Christ? *John 14:6 "Jesus said to him, 'I am the way, and the truth, and the life; no one comes to the Father but through Me.'" Revelation 3:20-21 "Behold, I stand at the door and knock; if anyone hears My voice and opens the door, I will come in to him, and will dine with him, and he with Me. He who overcomes, I will grant to him to sit down with Me on My throne, as I also overcame and sat down with My Father on His throne."*

My wonderment led me to probe God's heart for wisdom on how to reach those who declare they see no need to recognize Jesus as Savior. The world is full of people who do not believe that Jesus will be the very one who will either grant us permission to enter the throne room, or state that He does not know us. The results of that search will be found in the forthcoming pages as we journey through the Books of the Bible.

Our family became "The Ahrens Family Singers" when our children were still quite young. We cut our first 33 rpm album (that dates us) when our youngest child, Tim, was three years of age. The first song on the album was called "Oh, How I Love Jesus!" A portion of that particular version included us asking each child if they loved Jesus. Mom sang to the girls, Sherye (14) and Lori (11).

> Mom: "Hey Sherye, do you love Jesus?"
> Sherye: "Yes, I love Jesus!"
> Mom: "Do you really love Jesus?"
> Sherye: Yes, I really love Jesus?"
> Mom: "Tell me why do you love Jesus?"
> Sherye: "This is why I love Jesus, because He first loved me. I love Him! That is why I love Him!"

> > Then the whole family sings the chorus:
> > *"Oh, how I love Jesus! Oh, how I love Jesus!*
> > *Oh, how I love Jesus, because He first loved me!"*

> Mom: "Hey Lori, do you love Jesus?"
> Lori: "Yes, I love Jesus!"
> Mom: "Do you really love Jesus?"
> Lori: Yes, I really love Jesus?"
> Mom: "Tell me why do you love Jesus?"
> Lori: "This is why I love Jesus, because He first loved me. I love Him! That is why I love Him!" Then the whole family again sings the chorus of "Oh, How I Love Jesus!"

It was now Dad's turn to sing to his sons, John Jr. (8) and Tim (3) individually – and each of them responded. At age three – Tim had the most adorable little yodel in his voice when he sang, "This is why I love Jesus!" (I had to throw that in. Well – he <u>was</u> only 3. ☺) The song ended with Mom and Dad asking, *"Hey kids, do you love Jesus?"* followed by their response.

I remember a Jewish jeweler friend of ours, to whom we had given one of our albums, saying that the song made no sense to him at all. The phrase, "because He first loved me" *(I John 4:19,* which says, *"We love because He first loved us"),* to him meant absolutely nothing, as according to him, it was no different than any man falling in love with a woman and the girl saying, 'I love him because he first loved me.' I had to agree that in light of trying to help him understand why he needed to understand the need for Jesus as Savior, that phrase just was not enough.

Another incident I found to be difficult was when members of a different faith seemed to be unable to grasp the comprehension that Jesus was anything more than Someone who merely "showed the way" or was just "a good man!" There was no awareness on their part as to why there was a need for them to have a personal relationship with "Jesus." To them it made more sense to go directly to God, the Father. They found it unfamiliar to have to pray "in the name of Jesus," and claimed they were uncomfortable doing it.

There are also those who believed they would enter Heaven merely because they belonged to a particular denomination. They made it very clear that they were offended if anyone questioned their salvation. It would never occur to them that their sinful lifestyle would or could keep them out of Heaven, were they to never make Jesus the Lord of their lives. In their minds, their particular denominational church they attended was all they needed. I totally understood where they were coming from, as I recalled at the age of 8 asking someone what religion they were. My little heart sank to hear them stating that they belonged to a denomination I was not a part of. As that tender 8 year old, I felt sorry for them because I was absolutely positive that they would not be in Heaven with me. I did not realize that it was my denomination I was sold out to, not to Jesus Christ, nor did I understand what it meant to have a <u>relationship</u> with <u>Jesus</u>!

Lastly, there were those who claimed that their "religion" was very personal to them. They were determined that there was no need for them to have to be in a church in order to get to Heaven. They claimed that they could be out worshiping the earth for that matter and still be "spiritual." Well, it is true – the CHURCH is not our Savior, it is merely a haven for those who have a relationship with JESUS. However, it is that personal relationship with Jesus that assures our entry into Heaven. A church allows us to meet together and indefinitely helps build up the body of Christ when you pray together and share Christ's love with one another. There is nothing more fulfilling than when believers get together and share God's Word. Those who have had that experience can understand fully the meaning of "edification." God wants us to edify one another by sharing together, hence, the reason why we need "the church!"

For years I struggled with how to help those who did not have, want, or feel they needed a personal relationship with Jesus. For whatever reason, it was not natural for me to evangelize, as I did not seem to have an "Evangelistic" gift, though I envied those who did.

Hopefully, those who have had difficulty explaining to others the need for a personal relationship with Jesus will find this writing to bring a new understanding, and be a helpful aide in sharing Jesus, the most precious Gift of all.

Rev. Lynn Ahrens

— INTRODUCTION —

My goal in writing this book is to take you through the Bible and strive, in part, to illustrate the efforts that satan has made to keep mankind from ever being able to live with God the Father throughout eternity.

Once I came to the realization that the love of Jesus was greater than any love I had ever longed for or experienced in my life, my quest was to search out God's Word. Instead of reading the Bible from cover to cover, I found it easier to consume what God had to say by studying it "topically." Throughout the years, I've accumulated files on various subject matters such as "What does it mean to have a 'Covenant Relationship?'" "Healing Scriptures of the New Testament," "The Book of Revelation," "End Time Scriptures," "The Book of Hebrews and its Old Testament correlating Books," and "The Seven Feasts of God," to mention just a few.

Interestingly, while doing Biblical research over the years, I discovered a pattern weaving through the Old and New Testament scriptures. I also began to recognize that much of what Jesus said and taught in the four Gospels were actual quotes from the Old Testament. I discovered cycles or repetitions throughout the 66 books. This spurred my interest to research more. You could say that I acquired an addiction to delving into the Bible.

One day as I was meditating on the scenario in the Garden of Eden, I thought about the consequences that Adam <u>could</u> have changed had he taken the time to think through what he was about to do before actually acting on it. Knowing we all have made dim-witted decisions that cost us great heartache, my heart went out to him. Think about it. Adam COULD have turned the course of events and prevented the chaos the world has experienced from that time on as the result of his unfortunate decision.

As I perused this theme, it was interesting to find that each book of the Old Testament depicted satan's desperate attempts to corrupt all bloodlines in order to keep the Messiah from ever being born. Yet, from the beginning of time, satan was warned that he <u>will</u> be defeated despite any of those attempts or in spite of his minor "accomplishments."

The contexts of this writing come from my comprehension of the many years of note taking, listening to Godly teachings, and nourishing my own tenacity to consume God's Word. My goal is to share with you my child-like understanding of what transpired in the Garden, causing the havoc that has plagued mankind from then on. Should I, in bringing Scriptural references, not expound the meaning of <u>every</u> topic in a particular verse, it is because there are many authors who have adequately written books on those very subjects already.

In this book, my purpose is to focus on the need to understand the reason that Jesus is the only way to the Father. (It is totally impossible to bring you every attempt that is written in Scripture showing how satan has done all he could to turn all mankind against God. But my objective is to at least make you aware that he will never give up his quest until the time of that Great White Judgment Throne, at which point he will finally be cast into the "Lake of Fire" and experience his demise.)

There is coming a day when satan will have <u>no choice</u> but to <u>admit defeat</u>. In addition, AT *THE NAME OF JESUS,* he WILL also *BOW HIS KNEE,* and, whether he likes it or not, his *TONGUE <u>WILL</u> CONFESS THAT JESUS CHRIST IS LORD (Philippians 2:9-11).*

Hallelujah! Knowing this, it is imperative for each of us to recognize his feats, and then purpose to rise above them, overcoming all that he tries to deceive us with. Knowing the final outcome <u>should</u> bring us victory and peace.

Chapter One

— GOD CREATES MANKIND —

In Genesis 1:26, God states, "Let Us make man [Man Be] in Our image, according to Our likeness; and let them rule over the fish of the sea and over the birds of the sky and over the cattle and over all the earth, and over every creeping thing that creeps on the earth."

God's Plan "A" – God's desire was to create someone to fellowship with Him. So, Adam was created in God's image and likeness on the sixth day. Imagine the excitement as the angels witnessed this great phenomenon. They watched as God reached down, grabbed some red dirt in His hands and determined to create a being, which He then formed into an image and likeness of Himself. That meant that this man was like God in every way. The ONLY difference was the positions each had. The man's position was to rule the material earth, which God had just created. God's position, on the other hand, was to rule the Spiritual realm of the Universe.

Envision what the angels must have thought as they saw a form evolving, which actually looked to them like the very One Who was creating him. Here they saw wet clay taking the shape of a being that actually had parts - ears, nose, eyes, hair, arms, legs, etc. Wow! What a being! Then – to their amazement – this being walked, talked, and reasoned. (Ultimately, here was a perfect specimen, created in front of them who looked like God....as if he could have been His twin.) He was now a created being with the wisdom of God who had been given responsibilities which would honor anyone. However, God did not want a robot which HE would have to control, so He gave mankind the ability to <u>choose</u> to stay faithful to the One Who created them.

In the second chapter of Genesis, God explains how He created Adam, as well as telling us how He gave Adam the <u>authority to rule the earth</u>. One of the first responsibilities delegated to Adam was that of naming all the animals. God made it very clear to Adam that <u>everything</u> that once had been under God's authority was now under Adam's authority. God gave Adam a covenant gift that was to be his forever. (Not only was this gift for Adam, but for all mankind. Each descendant from Adam would be given the CHOICE to have that same covenant compensation, as well as God's authority.) Everything was based on CHOICE!

Chapter Two

— GOD GIVES ADAM AN OPPORTUNITY OF "CHOICE" —

In *Genesis 2:16-17,* God gave Adam an opportunity to prove himself faithful by letting him know there was the wonderful privilege of eating anything and everything in the Garden. There was only ONE command he had an obligation to obey. God commanded Adam not to eat of the *Tree of the Knowledge of Good and Evil. Genesis 2:16-17, "The LORD God commanded the man, saying, 'From any tree of the garden you may eat freely; but from the tree of the knowledge of good and evil you shall not eat, for in the day that you eat from it you will surely die.'"*

The whole earth belonged to Adam, except for that one tree. This should have seemed like a very simple thing to accept, since he had access to everything else he could or would have ever wanted or needed.

— LUCIFER'S COMPETETIVE ACTIONS —

Earlier, in Heaven, there had been a conflict of interest arising between God and Lucifer. It seems, according to *Isaiah 14*, that Lucifer, who was God's <u>Worship Leader,</u> and was also known as "The Day Star," or "The Shining Star," started a mutiny. He had decided that it was not enough for him to ONLY be known as God's main sidekick who led Worship. He wanted to BE God!

Obviously he stopped at nothing to try to wear God down in order for him to become Number 1. However, God is God, and He will not wear down. Yes, He will give every opportunity for a person to repent and be what he is called to be, but no one is able to wear God down.

Isaiah 14:11-20 quotes God as saying to Lucifer: "Your pomp and the music of your harps have been brought down to Sheol; Maggots are spread out as your bed beneath you and worms are your covering. How you have fallen from Heaven, O star of the morning, son of the dawn! You have been cut down to the earth, you who have weakened the nations!"

"But you said in your heart, 'I will ascend to Heaven; I will raise my throne above the stars of God, and I will sit on the mount of assembly in the recesses of the north. I will ascend above the heights of the clouds; I will make myself like the Most High.'"

"Nevertheless, you will be thrust down to Sheol, to the recesses of the pit. Those who see you will gaze at you, they will ponder over you, saying, 'Is this the man who made the earth tremble, who shook kingdoms, who made the world like a wilderness and overthrew its cities, who did not allow his prisoners to go home?'"

"All the kings of the nations lie in glory, each in his own tomb. But you have been cast out of your tomb like a rejected branch, clothed with the slain who are pierced with a sword, who go down to the stones of the pit like a trampled corpse".

"You will not be united with them in burial, because you have ruined your country, you have slain your people. May the offspring of evildoers not be mentioned forever!"

During this process, Lucifer was able to convince one-third of the angels to side with him. Unfortunately for Lucifer, the consequence was that he and all of his cohorts were literally thrown out of Heaven. At that time, God prepared the "Lake of Fire" [hell] that Lucifer and his fellow angels would ultimately end up in.

Revelation 12:9, "And the great dragon was thrown down, the serpent of old who is called the devil and satan, who deceives the whole world; he was thrown down to the earth, and his angels were thrown down with him."

God was not impressed with Lucifer's competitive spirit and unwillingness to relent. Therefore, God had no choice but to dispose of him. Lucifer had a choice to be submissive and enjoy the role that God had for him.... that of being God's number one angel.... leading worship, but he blew it....he rebelled.

Chapter Three

— WHAT EFFECT DID LUCIFERS FALL HAVE ON THIS EARTH? —

We see the answer to this question in *Isaiah 24:1-27*, which begins with, *"Behold, the LORD lays the earth waste, devastates it, distorts its surface and scatters its inhabitants..."* Isaiah shows us the Prophetic Word from God, declaring that God would have to destroy the earth and make it into waste land. In addition to that, it tells how the people would have to be scattered.

He then spells out the devastations the inhabitants of the earth would experience. How long? Throughout their life-time on this earth! For as long as satan [Lucifer] has opportunity to wreak havoc with God's people, doing what he can do, there will be a struggle.

— JUST WHO IS LUCIFER? —

Let us see what God tells us about Lucifer [satan] in *Ezekiel 28:12-19, "Son of man, take up a lamentation over the king of Tyre and say to him, 'Thus says the Lord GOD,' You had the seal of perfection, full of wisdom and perfect in beauty. You were in Eden, the garden of God; every precious stone was your covering: the ruby, the topaz and the diamond; the beryl, the onyx and the jasper; the lapis lazuli, the turquoise and the emerald; And the gold, the workmanship of your settings and sockets, was in you.'"*

"On the day that you were created, they were prepared. You were the anointed cherub who covers, and I placed you there. You were on the holy mountain of God; you walked in the midst of the stones of fire. You were blameless in your ways from the day you were created until unrighteousness was found in you."

"By the abundance of your trade you were internally filled with violence, and you sinned; Therefore, I have cast you as profane from the mountain of God. And I have destroyed you, O covering cherub, from the midst of the stones of fire. Your heart was lifted up because of your beauty; you corrupted your wisdom by reason of your splendor."

"I cast you to the ground; I put you before kings, that they may see you. By the multitude of your iniquities, in the unrighteousness of your trade you profaned your sanctuaries. Therefore I have brought fire from the midst of you; it has consumed you, and I have turned you to ashes on the earth in the eyes of all who see you. All who know you among the peoples are appalled at you; you have become terrified and you will cease to be forever.'"

Chapter Four

— ADAM AND EVE'S AUTHORITATIVE DEMISE —

Now, we begin to see how Lucifer was not about to accept being thrown out of Heaven without a fight, nor was he satisfied with taking "no" for an answer. We see in *Genesis 3*, his manipulative plan to retaliate by trying to attain the authority over the earth, that self-same authority which God had previously given to <u>Adam.</u>

At the end of *Genesis* an interesting phenomenon unfolded before the watchful eyes of the Angels who had been delighted to observe the creation of Adam. God's creative work was done within the first six days. On the seventh day, He rested. On the eighth day, God looked at Adam and saw what was hidden in him that needed to come out of him – someone for Adam to love! *Genesis 2:20-22, "...But for Adam there was not found a helper suitable for him. So the LORD God caused a deep sleep to fall upon the man, and he slept; then He took one of his ribs, and closed up the flesh at that place. And the LORD God fashioned into a woman the rib which He had taken from the man, and brought her to the man."*

This "woman" was to be Adam's helpmate, his beloved companion and counterpart. She was not created, but was formed from Adam's rib, taken from his side. Remember, back in the first chapter when God created man – He stated, *"male and female created He them"* and *"they shall have dominion..." Genesis 1:27*

Gene Edwards describes in his book, *"100 Days in the Secret Place,"* how Adam was ONE – and now there would be TWO. However, the nature of God is to be ONE. Therefore, the TWO, man and woman, must be ONE again [marriage]. His substance was divided, yet it remains the same. She is OF him, FROM him, and ONE WITH him. Yet, they are separate. (This would be an excellent book to read for greater understanding.)

Because the woman came from man, man is to be the one to pour out his love towards the woman.... wooing her, to which she then tenderly responds. Wow! Isn't it amazing how it makes sense why women have been drawn to men all along? It is ONLY NATURAL for the woman to return to where she had been previously HIDDEN. No wonder she has always responded lovingly and passionately to tender loving caresses from her man.

In *Genesis 3:20,* Eve was to be known as the mother of all people. *"Now the man [Adam] called his wife Eve, because she was the mother of all the living."* In *Genesis 2:23,* Adam, when receiving her from God, exclaims, "Wow, at last!" (Lynn's paraphrased version ☐). Nonetheless, the Bible actually says, *"The man said, 'this is now bone of my bones and flesh of my flesh; she shall be called woman, because she was taken out of man.'"* He loved her dearly and was most pleased with this precious gift he had received from God.

God had given Adam everything, except for <u>that tree</u>. In actuality, of all that Adam could see, as well as what he could not see, the ONLY restriction was that Adam was not to eat of the "Tree of the Knowledge of Good and Evil." God was permitting Adam the opportunity to use FREE CHOICE, rather than be robotically moved.

Now, let us take a look at what satan was thinking. He recognized that God had transferred all of His authority to Adam, and NOT to him. Imagine his mind spinning. His ultimate purpose was to connive his way back into what he sought after, while still in Heaven as God's worship leader.... to be "Number 1." If he could not conquer dominion in Heaven, then the thing he would have to do was try his level best to obtain ownership of the earth.

Satan was the one who now moved on to plan "B." Plan "A" for him was to try to conquer possession of Heaven, but we read that he failed miserably. He knew what God had told Adam about that tree. He had to purpose to take advantage of the fact that Eve was not there when God spoke to Adam and never heard it explained by God.

Nevertheless, we can assume that Adam must have told Eve what God said, based on her response to satan when he questioned her on it. *Genesis 3:1* states, *"Now the serpent was more crafty than any beast of the field that the LORD God had made."* Verse 1 informs us that satan smugly challenged Eve by means of questioning her integrity when he said, *"Indeed, has God said, 'You shall not eat from any tree of the garden?'"* To which Eve replied in verse 2-3, *"From the fruit of the trees of the garden we may eat; but from the fruit of the tree which is in the middle of the garden, God has said, 'you shall not eat from it or touch it, lest you die.'"*

We can see here that confusion must have already set in, based on her response. Perhaps she was nervous, due to the challenge satan was throwing at her, or she might have misunderstood what Adam told her. Perhaps, because he was a man, Adam merely stuck to the FACTS, and expected her to understand what he did not say.

In any case, according to the record, God never said to Adam that they were not allowed to touch the "Tree of the

Knowledge of Good and Evil." If we go back to *Genesis 2:16-17,* we can see the actual words God spoke. *"And the LORD God commanded the man, saying, 'From any tree of the garden you may eat freely; but from the tree of the knowledge of good and evil you shall not eat, for in that day that you eat from it you shall surely die.'"*

Obviously, satan was trying to wear Eve down by telling her that she surely would not die, but, she would instead become <u>like God</u> if she would eat of the fruit. This is a direct lie, (the first one listed in scripture). Not ONLY that, satan embellished and glorified eating the fruit even more by telling her she would know the difference between good and evil. *Genesis 3:5 says, "For God knows that in that day you eat from it your eyes will be opened, and you will be like God, knowing good and evil."* Sadly, she crumbled under the pressure and ate the fruit.

In retrospect, obviously satan knew better than to dare approach Adam, whom God had given all of His authority, to try and deceive him, but instead took the coward's way and accosted Eve. One has to wonder how Eve could possibly be convinced into believing this "snake" that happens to appear out of nowhere. Until now, she had lived in an environment of love, peace, and comfort, not to mention having had intimate fellowship with God. Eve had never identified with rejection, abuse, or lies, so one has to wonder how satan could sway her to suddenly believe God was a liar. Somehow he was able to get her to ignore everything she HAD and focus on that ONE tree, turning her mind into thinking God was a TAKER, instead of the GIVER that He really is. Was she thinking there was something in that tree God was withholding from her? It makes one wonder how she could have been so deceived to no longer believe the God whom she had trusted until now.

— WHERE WAS ADAM WHEN ALL THIS HAPPENED? —

Regardless of whether Adam was right there hearing all of the conversation or not, the fact remains that he was still the <u>final authority</u>, as he knew what God had commanded of him. I am sure Adam must have found himself in a conundrum, knowing that the woman whom he so dearly loved had just blown it. He, at this point, had a heart wrenching decision to make. If he chose the woman he loved with all his being, and ate of the fruit she had just offered him, he would have to give up all that God had given to him. However, if he opted for God, he would have to be separated from this beloved, precious gift, whom God had formed out of his side, as she had already taken a bite from the forbidden fruit offered by Lucifer.

Unfortunately, it appears that he never really thought it through, nor did he seem to understand all the consequences. For had he truly searched his heart and used his authority to rebuke satan rather than giving in to him, he would have realized that though he may have lost Eve, God would have given him so much more for his faithfulness.

We need to recognize that Adam had a spirit, a soul, and a body. He was created to make decisions. God never intended to have robots. He freely gave mankind the CHOICE to be faithful. Regrettably, Adam's decision was made with his soul (mind, will and emotion) rather than with his spirit. The second he ate from the forbidden fruit, all the authority God had ever given to him, in that moment, was handed over to satan. No turning back! It was a done deal! Satan now had acquired all authority over all the earth. High treason [betrayal] had been committed by Adam.

In actuality, Adam "sold out" to satan. That precious commodity which had been given to him by God he now handed over to satan, to do with as he pleased. Satan now had in his control <u>all power</u> to corrupt the earth in any way

37

he pleased. Since he hated God with a passion, what else would he do but endeavor to destroy everything that God had made!

Chapter Five

— WHAT IS THE MEANING OF ADAM COMMITTING HIGH TREASON? —

Adam's high treason meant that he and Eve were no longer protected from evil. Their eyes were definitely now opened to understanding the difference between <u>good and evil</u>. *Genesis 3:7.* *"Then the eyes of both of them were opened, and they knew that they were naked; and they sewed fig leaves together and made themselves loin coverings."*

Yet, life was different from what they had expected, especially after relying on what satan promised Eve in *verse 5 saying, "For God knows that in the day you eat from it your eyes will be opened, and you will be like God, knowing good and evil."*

This meant they no longer had that special, intimately close relationship with God they once had. And, no longer would they feel that same <u>love</u> relationship. Instead, shame became its replacement. Adam and Eve would obviously now feel the evil more than the good.

Imagine what a disappointment those two must have felt to have walked with God, to have been given the authority to name all the animals that God had created, to talk with God, to laugh with Him any time of the day or night, ONLY to now have a wedge placed between them and their most intimate "Friend."

Obviously, Adam and Eve were greatly affected as *Genesis 3:7-8* tells us that they heard God coming and quickly hid themselves from Him. *"Then the eyes of both of them were opened, and they realized they were naked; so they sewed fig leaves together and made coverings for themselves. And they heard the sound of the LORD God walking in the garden in the cool of the day, and the man and his wife hid themselves from the presence of the LORD God among the trees of the garden."*

Before, they only knew <u>mentally</u> what sin was. but now they knew from <u>experience</u>. Adam and Eve had lost <u>God-consciousness</u>, and gained <u>self-consciousness</u>. They lost the power to do good and gained the power to do evil.

Because of disobedience, their relationship with God and Adam's position of authority was severed. As a result, God had no choice but to have his angels escort Adam and Eve out of the Garden of Eden before they could possibly touch "The Tree of Life." *Genesis 3:22 - Then the LORD God said, "Behold, the man has become like one of Us, knowing good and evil; and now, he might stretch out his hand, and take also from the tree of life, and eat, and live forever"* — God could not take the chance of them getting anywhere <u>near</u> the "Tree of Life," for the reason that should they even touch THIS tree, they would then be doomed to live in their <u>sinful state</u> forever.

In summary, God had given to Adam the SAME authority that God Himself had. This authority meant that Adam could do whatever God was capable of doing. Therefore, satan hoodwinked Eve into doing the ONE thing that God had commanded Adam NOT to allow to happen. Adam was placed in charge of everything and anything that happened on earth. Remember that Adam HAD the CHOICE of rebuking satan and keeping his God-given authority over him.

In spite of this, Adam's heartstrings for Eve obviously overpowered, for that moment, his trust in God. <u>In that split second, he made the gravest mistake ever, which caused havoc for the rest of mankind. Adam now lost everything and all who would be born into this earth would feel the consequences of his choice.</u>

In essence, satan now felt most confident that he finally held the reigns. He felt arrogantly secure that he was now able to do whatever he wanted to do. He was smugly thinking God could do <u>nothing</u> about it, since the authority was now his and no longer belonged to God.

As we walk through the books of the Bible, satan's strategies are clear as he tries to make sure <u>no one</u> would ever be able to live with God – FOREVER! We see how he is doing everything in his power to make sure that if he was to be doomed to the "Lake of Fire," then so would all mankind. We will also see in these forthcoming books how God reveals that it was to be His Son, Jesus Christ, who was to be the coming "Messiah" and the One Who redeemed all people back to God.

Chapter Six

— IT IS GOD WHO NOW MUST
GO TO PLAN "B" —

Because Adam committed high treason in the Garden by selling out to satan, God could have lost everything. God now needed to devise a plan whereby He could <u>gain back the lost</u> – those whom He had created for His glory. *Isaiah 43:7 says, "Everyone who is called by My Name, and whom I have created for My glory, whom I have formed, even whom I have made."*

At that point in time, anyone who was to be born into this earth had no chance of spending eternity with God, nor could he have had any kind of a relationship with God, the Father. As it is, satan and his cohorts, who had all been thrown out of Heaven, were told that there was a "Lake of Fire" prepared just for them. That "Lake of Fire" was to become their ever-lasting domain. Hence, unless God did something drastic, all offspring from Adam and Eve would end up there as well.

Satan's essential plan was to make sure that if he and his cohorts were destined to go to the "Lake of Fire", then he would do whatever it took to make sure he took every one else with him. Remember, his goal was to make sure no one

EVER gets to reside with God in Heaven, since he never will.

Clarification note: Yes, quite clearly, God is an all-knowing God. The fact that I have used the expressions Plan "A" and Plan "B" in trying to clarify the sequence of events could easily be misinterpreted and a bit controversial. However, I would like to make it clear that I am not implying that God did not know what He was doing. It is my intention to merely bring out the fact that God's original plan was to create someone like Him who would reside and have fellowship with Him forever, I simply called that Plan "A." Because God created Adam with the ability to make choices in life, God needed to have a Plan "B" in the event Adam made the wrong choice, and, therefore, is really nothing more than a clarification issue that made sense to me and I pray it will make sense to you as well.

— THE LOST —

What does the phrase, "the lost" mean? Why does God have to gain back "the lost?" Who is it that is lost?

Prior to committing this treachery by purposely disobeying God, by eating of the forbidden fruit in the Garden of Eden, Adam and Eve had been clothed in righteousness. At the instant of Adam's disobedience, God had to clothe both of them in fig leaves, as now they saw themselves as naked and they were ashamed. Now, they were "lost" from God, as all of mankind would be.

Sin had now consumed both of them. As a result of this, from this day forward, their offspring would also be born into SIN. This is the "sin of the world" which is spoken of throughout the Scriptures. This SIN (that Jesus died for) was the very same sin that Adam had forced upon all mankind with his unfaithfulness, when he joined his beloved woman eating the forbidden fruit.

The problem of satan having total control and full authority over the earth meant that anyone now born into this world ultimately became subject to satan's control. <u>Unless</u> God found a way to redeem Adam, Eve, and any offspring they would have, every single being would end up in the "Lake of Fire." It is important to note again that hell was meant ONLY for satan and his fallen angels. However, in this sinful state, <u>not one</u> child born could have access to God, the Father, and be able to live with Him in eternity.

<u>God's Plan "B"</u> – So, what was God to do? In *Genesis 3:14-15* we see His Plan "B" going into action. God questioned Adam and Eve as to why they disobeyed Him. Then, God divulged His plans to bring about the redemption that would turn the course of events. He also expounded the demise of the enemy. *"The LORD God said to the serpent, because you have done this, cursed are you more than all cattle, and more than every beast of the field; On your belly you will go, and dust you will eat all the days of your life; and I will put enmity between you and the woman, and between your seed and her seed; He shall bruise you on the head, and you shall bruise him on the heel."* In hindsight, centuries passed before seeing the fruition of God's efforts.

Chapter Seven

— THE CURSE AND THE PROMISE —
(Each curse was twofold)

To the serpent: In *Genesis 3:14*, God is speaking to satan, telling him what He would have to do as a result of satan having deluded Adam and Eve. The Bible says, *"The LORD God said to the serpent, 'Because you have done this, cursed are you more than all cattle, and more than every beast of the field; On your belly you will go, and dust you will eat all the days of your life.'"* This statement shows us that God is convinced that His Plan "B" would, without a doubt, be fulfilled.

Satan's Curse: Not only was the serpent [satan] being directly cursed with a physical curse, but also was promised that he would ultimately be crushed by the Seed of the woman. God promised that He would carry out the decree through the Seed of the woman (Christ came as the fulfillment of that promise through the Virgin Mary). Christ would utterly crush and defeat satan. The ONLY thing satan can possibly do is to merely inflict temporary sufferings onto the Messiah. The victory of Christ was a direct crushing of satan in fulfillment of this curse, for it was satan who was behind the serpent in Eden.

<u>To the Woman</u>: *Genesis 3:16, "To the woman he said, 'I will greatly multiply your pain in childbearing; in pain you shall bring forth children, yet your desire shall be for your husband, and he shall rule over you.'"*

<u>The Woman's Curse</u>: The woman receives the penalty of her actions. The conflict between the man and the woman, predicted in the words "desire" and "rule," meant there would be a strain regarding man's ruling and dominance over the woman. Relationships now would be strained to pandemonium, all as a result of Adam's sin. The consequences for women also include suffering great pain in childbirth. The ONLY means of fulfilling God's promise to crush the serpent's head with the heel of someone born to a woman would be through the child bearing suffering of a woman.

<u>To Adam</u>: *Genesis 3:17, "Then to Adam he said, 'Because you have listened to the voice of your wife, and have eaten from the tree about which I commanded you, saying, You shall not eat of it, cursed is the ground because of you; in toil you shall eat of it all the days of your life; Both thorns and thistles it shall grow for you; and you shall eat the plants of the field. By the sweat of your face you shall eat bread till you return to the ground, because from it you were taken; For you are dust, and to dust you shall return.'"*

<u>Adam's Curse</u>: Adam's consequence was that the earth would be cursed causing toil and frustration for humanity. It is not <u>*work*</u> that will be the result of the curse, but it will be <u>toil and frustration</u>. Another result of Adam's sin was physical death. In *Romans 5:14-15, "Nevertheless death reigned from Adam until Moses, even over those who had not sinned in the likeness of the offense of Adam, who is a type of Him who was to come. But the free gift is not like the transgression. For if by the transgression of the one the many died, much more did the grace of God and the gift by the grace of the one Man, Jesus Christ, abound to the many."* Paul states here that all death was rooted in Adam's sin.

The issue of Adam and Eve's shame at their nakedness confirmed the split between man and woman. They were no longer the original and pure <u>one flesh</u> that God had created them to be. God had to clothe them. By doing so, God gave them the knowledge they had definitely caused a future of pandemonium for all mankind. Imagine the shame that they must have felt!

Adam exercised faith and hope by calling the woman "Eve," because she would be the mother of all. He looked to the life that she would bring forth. Adam and Eve now hoped in the promise that someone born to her would undo the curse they had caused by their disobedience. However, Adam and Eve were totally oblivious as to <u>Who</u> this child would be or <u>when</u> this Child would appear. That promised One would ultimately be Jesus, the Christ, born of the Virgin Mary.

Chapter Eight

— A GENERAL SYNOPSIS TO CLARIFY WHAT HAS HAPPENED THUS FAR —

L ucifer was God's worship leader in Heaven before the earth was ever created. Because he was not satisfied with his position and wanted to be GOD, he started a mutiny. He astoundingly was able to convince 1/3 of the angels in Heaven to join in this rebellion. Because of this insurrection, God had no choice but to throw satan and his cohorts out of Heaven.

In the Garden of Eden, satan succeeded in causing Adam's disloyalty. Thus, ALL AUTHORITY was transferred into satan's hands – and out of God's hands. Had God not gone to Plan "B", ALL offspring would have had no choice but to go to the "Lake of Fire," which was originally created for satan and his cohorts only. NOT ONE SOUL would be able to spend eternity with God in Heaven.

In order for anyone to enter into God's Throne Room for time without end, God had to devise a plan where He could, at the right moment in time, provide a man Child who was from a pure bloodline, Who would turn the tide. This Child would have to be sinless. He would ultimately be required to take all of what had happened in the Garden of Eden and rectify it by shedding His own blood, taking upon Himself the sins of the world from the beginning of time.

The Bible gives an example of what the Messiah would have to do. In the Book of *Leviticus,* chapter *16,* we see the High Priests using the <u>Perfect Male Goats</u> who become SIN OFFERINGS for ATONEMENT. *Leviticus 16:20-22, "When Aaron has finished making atonement for the Most Holy Place, the Tent of Meeting, and the altar, he shall bring forward the live goat. He is to lay both hands on the head of the live goat and confess over it all the wickedness and rebellion of the Israelites—all their sins—and put them on the goat's head. He shall send the goat away into the desert in the care of a man appointed for the task. The goat will carry on itself all their sins to a solitary place; and the man shall release it in the desert."*

For clarification, one goat was to be slaughtered; the other was to be sent into the wilderness, a land that was uninhabited, carrying the sins. This was to be a representation of Christ removing all sins from mankind as far as the east is from the west, and remembering them no more. *Psalm 103:12; "As far as the east is from the west, so far has he removed our transgressions from us."* Hebrews *13:17 "Obey your leaders and submit to them; for they keep watch over your souls, as those who will give an account. Let them do this with joy and not with grief, for this would be unprofitable for you."*

As you read the books of the Old Testament, you will see that the Bible speaks of many people just like you and I who have endured difficulties, which the enemy had thrown in their paths. We may think that we are the ONLY ones who constantly have to endure trials and tribulations, feeling overwhelmed by these attacks that seem so constant. But we hear of many who have given powerful examples of how they overcame the challenges of their plights.

Look at those who overcame many of the enemy's tactics: In Genesis we see Noah, Abraham, Sarah, Jacob, and Joseph; In Exodus we read of Moses, Aaron, Miriam, and the Children of Israel; In Numbers and Judges we are introduced to Gideon, Barak, and Samson; In Samuel it is David and Samuel; and then, we study about all the Prophets of Old. Like all of them, we have certain dilemmas that we can successfully overcome. On the other hand, we find that particular state of affairs is not as readily solved. However, we are taught throughout the Scriptures to be persistent and never give up.

Chapter Nine

— THE CREDENCE OF THE BIBLE! —

S ome have stated that the Bible being the "inspired Word of God" really only meant that it was written by people just like us, who felt inspired to give their own opinions and viewpoints of what happened. They claim that the Bible is filled with mistakes and definitely not relevant to our modern world. This concept only brings confusion to the reader. It also proves that whoever suggests such a thought, obviously has never read the entire Bible to see how themes and types weave in and out throughout its 66 books. The Old Testament had concealed that which the New Testament has revealed.

Yes, we need to "rightly divide" the Word of God. In *2 Timothy 2:15*, Paul tells us to *"Study to shew thyself approved unto God, a workman that needeth not to be ashamed, rightly dividing the word of truth."* What this means is that we need to know the difference between what was accurately spoken and what was not. You already had opportunity to see one example, in Genesis 2, where satan lies to Eve and tells her she would become wiser after eating of the forbidden fruit.

One other example is *Job 1:20-21* which states, *"Then Job arose and tore his robe and shaved his head, and he fell to the ground and worshiped. He said, 'Naked I came from my mother's womb, and naked I shall return there the LORD gave and the LORD has taken away....'"* The truth is that God is not the one who sends diseases and kills people. Instead, that is the strategy of the enemy [satan]. *John 10:10* quotes Jesus as saying, *"The thief* [satan] *comes only to steal and kill and destroy; I came that they* [Christians] *may have life, and have it abundantly."*

A remarkable evidence of fulfilled prophecy is just one case in point. Hundreds of Bible prophecies have been fulfilled, specifically and meticulously, often long after the Prophet has died. An example would be Daniel, the Prophet, who predicted many years before Christ was born, that Jesus would be the One to come as Israel's Promised Messiah. *Daniel 9:24-27.*

Each of the four Gospel writers gave a very detailed account of the happenings between the Birth of Christ and His resurrection, yet each spoke precisely to a specific audience. Hence, the reason why each Gospel writer would not need to address everyone in the same fashion! As you would expect from multiple biographies of one particular person, each biography is bound to have variations of style, yet there is agreement in the facts.

We know the authors were not simply making these things up, as the Gospels do offer geographical names and cultural details that have been confirmed by historians and archaeologists. Still, some different information was given in the four Gospels to reach and relate to the different audiences whom the Gospels were meant to reach.

The New Testament was written after 400 years of silence after the book of Malachi, when an Angel proclaimed the news of the birth of John the Baptist, who would be the forerunner of Jesus, the prophesied Messiah.

Chapter Ten

— BACK TO GENESIS —
— AWARE OF GOD'S PLAN "B," SATAN
BEGINS HIS STRATEGIES —

Adam and Eve had no clue which of their offspring was meant to become the chosen One. Nor had they any hint as to <u>when</u> God was going to fulfill the promises of regaining the authority that satan so pompously delighted in possessing. On the other hand, neither did satan know Who it would be or when He would be born.

— CAIN KILLS ABEL —

We see in *Genesis 4* the beginning of satan's mission. He began his course of action by bringing strife between Cain and Abel, which ended in Abel's death. "Cha-ching! One out of the way," says satan! However, *Genesis 4:10-12* says, *"And the LORD said, 'What have you done? The voice of your brother's blood is crying to me from the ground. And now you are cursed from the ground, which has opened its mouth to receive your brother's blood from your hand. When you cultivate the ground, it shall no longer yield its strength to you; you shall be a vagrant and a wanderer on the earth.'"*

Because he murdered Abel, Cain was corrupted and cursed. As a result, neither he nor his offspring could be the Savior of mankind. We have to remember that the Redeemer MUST come from a sinless, pure bloodline.

Adam and Eve would have more children, and though two children were out of his way, satan knew he had to be crafty in order to not allow this "Messiah" to come to fruition. As the population grew, he devised several plans to try to keep God from ever allowing that pure bloodline to become a reality.

— SONS OF GOD COME INTO THE DAUGHTERS OF MEN —

In Genesis 6:1-7, as the human population increased rapidly, satan decides that he would have the sons of god come together with the beautiful daughters of men. *"Now it came about, when men began to multiply on the face of the land, and daughters were born to them, that the sons of God saw that the daughters of men were beautiful; and they took wives for themselves, whomever they chose."*

"Then the LORD said, 'My Spirit shall not strive with man forever, because he also is flesh; nevertheless his days shall be one hundred and twenty years.' The Nephilim [giants] were on the earth in those days, and also afterward, when the sons of God came in to the daughters of men, and they bore children to them. Those were the mighty men who were of old, men of renown."

"Then the LORD saw that the wickedness of man was great on the earth, and that every intent of the thoughts of his heart was ONLY evil continually. The LORD was sorry that He had made man on the earth, and He was grieved in His heart. The LORD said, 'I will blot out man whom I have

created from the face of the land, from man to animals to creeping things and to birds of the sky; for I am sorry that I have made them.'"

— WHO WERE THESE SO CALLED "SONS OF GOD?" —

Over the years, I remember hearing three different views:

- Satan's cohorts – the fallen angels
- Cain's male offspring
- Pre-flood giants

Whoever they were, the offspring they created were giants, and thus they generated an impure bloodline. In verse 6, God actually says that He was sorry that He had ever created mankind, and it broke His heart to see what was happening. Remember, satan's goal was to corrupt all bloodlines, giving God no chance to bring forth that Promised Messiah who had to come from a pure lineage.

Chapter Eleven

— NOAH'S SONS: SHEM, HAM, JAPHETH —

The earth had become corrupt and filled with violence, but God found a man who was righteous in His sight. Beginning in *Genesis 6:8-14*, we see how God had to stop the corruption by wiping out the populace. *"But Noah found favor in the eyes of the LORD. These are records of the generations of Noah. Noah was a righteous man, blameless in his time; Noah walked with God. And Noah became the father of three sons, Shem, Ham, and Japheth."*

"Now the earth was corrupt in the sight of God, and the earth was filled with violence. And God looked on the earth, and behold, it was corrupt; for all flesh had corrupted their way upon the earth. Then God said to Noah, 'the end of all flesh has come before me; for the earth is filled with violence because of them; and behold, I am about to destroy them with the earth. Make yourself an ark of gopher wood; you shall make the ark with rooms, and cover it inside and out with pitch.'"

God spoke to Noah and informed him of His need for an Ark. God asked Noah to build a boat based on clear-cut specifications that He would give to him. Due to the corruption that had occurred, God had no choice but to wipe out the entire race in order to stop the current impure bloodline.

A flood was not only <u>unheard of</u> in that day, due to the earth being watered by a <u>mist;</u> it was also inconceivable to comprehend how it <u>could rain</u>, much less, how water <u>could cover the earth.</u>

Some have asked me why God would be so cruel and inconsiderate as to destroy innocent little children, especially babies. The problem is, the babies conceived by parents of an impure bloodline would obviously not have pure blood, therefore would ultimately be the carriers and spreaders of that DNA. God had <u>no choice</u> but to dispose of <u>all</u> impurities, which <u>had</u> to include the babies.

The ONLY individuals that were now left on the entire earth after the flood consisted of Noah, his three sons, and their wives. Consequently, EIGHT people were left to live on the earth with the animals that had been placed in the Ark. It has been questioned as to whether or not all the animals could even FIT into the Ark. Since it was recorded as being a fact, if God said it, why would we doubt it? Scholars have mentioned that it does make sense and is indeed a possibility if all the animals were very young, thus very tiny.

From these three sons of Noah came all of mankind now scattered across the earth. In reading *Genesis 9 and 10,* we find satan continuing his line of stratagem again by attacking and corrupting one of Noah's sons – Ham – who ended up being cursed for what he had done to his father.

Chapter Twelve

— THE TOWER OF BABEL —

Beginning in *Genesis 11:1-9* we see how satan used Ham's descendants to build a tower in Babel that was to reach into the Heavens. This was meant to turn the focus away from God. *"Now the whole earth used the same language and the same words. It came about as they journeyed east, that they found a plain in the land of Shinar and settled there.*

They said to one another, "Come, let us make bricks and burn them thoroughly." And they used brick for stone, and they used tar for mortar. They said, "Come, let us build for ourselves a city, and a tower whose top will reach into Heaven, and let us make for ourselves a name, otherwise we will be scattered abroad over the face of the whole earth."

"The LORD came down to see the city and the tower which the sons of men had built. The LORD said, "Behold, they are one people, and they all have the same language. And this is what they began to do, and now nothing which they purpose to do will be impossible for them. Come, let Us go down and there confuse their language, so that they will not understand one another's speech. So the LORD scattered

them abroad from there over the face of the whole earth; and they stopped building the city."

"Therefore its name was called Babel, because there the LORD confused the language of the whole earth; and from there the LORD scattered them abroad over the face of the whole earth."

Everyone spoke the same language up to this point. However, God knew that if they were able to accomplish their goal due to their common language and unity, there was nothing that would become impossible for them to accomplish. He had to channel them away from satan's tactics.

Consequently, God chose to give them different languages so that they would no longer be able to understand one another. For this reason, the people were scattered all over the earth. This ended the building of the tower in the city of Babel. The word "Babel" has the Greek translation, meaning "confusion." Satan lost this one as well! Hallelujah!

Chapter Thirteen

— THE CALL OF ABRAM —

G od needed to find someone who could truly be sold out to Him and be willing to make a covenant (a <u>binding</u> pledge or agreement) with Him. So, God went to a place called UR (modern day Iraq). There He asked a man named Abram to pick up his family and his belongings, leave his pagan relatives who worshipped idols, and with no questions asked, expected him to "go where He sends him."

Abram had experienced no other culture except that which he was brought up in, and this way of life included the worship of idols. Yet, there seemed to arise in Abram a trust in this God who was foreign to him, but who, at that moment, was asking him to do the unbelievable.

I can just see his Mom asking, "Abram, <u>where</u> is it that you are going?" With Abram replying, "Don't know! But, the One Who has asked me to go said that if I set off to the land that He will show me, He would make me the father of a great nation. If I do this, He will bless those who bless me, curse those who curse me, and get this, <u>all</u> the families of the earth will be blessed through me. So, how can I not go for it?"

As a result of these promises, Abram decided to trust this God and henceforth, took Sarai, his wife; Lot, his nephew; all the livestock, including the families and servants of both; and proceeded to head for Haran, to see his uncle. From there, Abram headed on to his ultimate destination, which was the area that was occupied by the Canaanites. God had promised him that all that land was to become his.

Genesis 12 tells us that there was a famine in the area. So, Abram took his family down to Egypt to wait it out. While on their way, Abram and Sarai got into this conversation about the danger of going to Egypt. Abram proceeded to inform Sarai of an important reality that he had heard of, concerning Egyptians having a history of stealing wives and then killing the husbands. So he begged her to lie and declare that she was his sister. He did not want to die, he wanted his life spared.

Sure enough, the very thing they had discussed happened (another sly trick of satan to try to stop God from completing His mission). Apparently Sarai was a very beautiful woman, and Pharaoh was the culprit who saw Sarai and had her brought into his chambers. However, God stepped in and sent a plague upon Pharaoh's household, scaring the daylights out of him. He quickly gave Sarai back to Abram and sent them out of the country, under security escort, no less! A most interesting plot on satan's part to again try to corrupt the bloodline! On the other hand, to no avail...again! It backfired on him!

— SARAI HAS ABRAM IMPREGNATE HAGAR —

Genesis 15-16: By now, God had made a covenant with Abram, promising him a son. Yet up to this point, Sarai had no children. As the years went by and there was no sign of that promised son, Sarai decided to "help" God by having her husband lay with her servant girl, Hagar. It was the custom in that culture for a barren woman to be allowed to give her husband to her concubine in order to gain an heir, as well as to ease the pain of humiliation for not having a child of her own. However, this was not God's plan. Yet, nine months later Hagar had a son and named him Ishmael.

Unfortunately, havoc broke out when Sarai, the very one who had coerced this whole thing, became jealous of Hagar, and Hagar became quite spiteful and pompous. She began rubbing in the fact that she was the one who had Abram's child, not Sarai....a very hurtful scenario.

Satan's strategy did not work here either. Quite possibly, he might have thought that Abram and Sarai would give up after Ishmael was born, as they had reached their "winter" years, and could have though that it was too late for them. Later we will see what really happened!

Chapter Fourteen

— LOT AND HIS DAUGHTERS —

After the famine, Abram, his entire family, and livestock returned from Egypt to the land that God had promised him. By this time their livestock and families had grown. Lot's servants and Abram's servants were experiencing family strife to the utmost.

Abram saw that it would be a detriment for the family to stay together, and asked Lot to choose whatever part of the country he would like for him and his family, as well as his servants to live in. Lot looked around and greedily chose what looked to be the most luscious countryside. That beautiful area was called the Jordan Valley.

Sodom and Gomorrah were a part of the region which Lot had chosen. In *Genesis 18-19*, homosexuality was prominent in the two cities and God was displeased with what was happening, and therefore had no choice but to destroy them. Though the land was once luxuriously green with foliage, after its destruction, the region remained barren, brown, and desolate. *Genesis 18:20* states, *"And the LORD said, 'the outcry of Sodom and Gomorrah is indeed great, and their sin is exceedingly grave,'"* meaning that homosexuality was and still is an abomination to the Lord; as He does not change

His mind! *Numbers 23:19-20.* *"God is not a man, that He should lie; nor a son of man, that He should repent; Has He said, and will He not do it? Or has He spoken, and will He not make it good? Behold, I have received a command to bless; when He has blessed, then I cannot revoke it."*

Later we see Abram pleading with God on behalf of Lot's family. After a bit of debate between God and Abram, it was finally agreed upon that if Abram found even 10 righteous people in Sodom and Gomorrah, then God would spare the cities. However, in the end, not even 10 could be found who wanted to leave.

Interestingly, though Lot, his wife, and his two daughters were all spared being burned with the towns, they actually had to be <u>forcibly</u> removed. Lot and his family had gotten so caught up in the sin of Sodom and Gomorrah, and that sin had gotten so ingrained in them, that the Angels whom God had sent to remove them had to literally DRAG them out.

The Angels warned them not to look back towards the city as they went. Nevertheless, Lot's wife could not resist, and she did indeed turn to look, at which point she turned into a pillar of salt. Here again, satan had decided to pull another one of his shenanigans. You see, at this moment in time, he was still not sure whom God was going to choose to use to bring forth that Promised Messiah. He could not take a chance in <u>anyone</u> being successful in bringing forth that One Who would take all authority away from him, and give it back to God, where it belonged.

Starting at *Genesis 19:30,* we are informed that Lot's daughters still had soul ties to their former environment! Because Lot was afraid to move to Zoar, he and his two daughters lived in a cave. Scripture says, *"...he was afraid of the people there."* The daughters now became fearful that they would never have any children...thinking there would be no men for them to choose from. After all, for all they knew, they could be the only "3" people left on earth.

With a little manipulation the daughters got their father drunk – had intercourse with him – and each girl ended up pregnant with their father's children. The one daughter had a son and called him Moab, who became the ancestor of the Moabites. The second daughter named her son Ben-ammi, who became the ancestor of the Ammonites. Both became the enemies of Israel and would remain so. Seemingly, satan's tactics worked with these two.

Chapter Fifteen

— THE BEGINNING OF THE "PURE" BLOODLINE, THROUGH ABRAHAM —

In *Genesis 15:5,* God asks Abram to go out *"And He took him outside and said, 'Now look toward the Heavens, and count the stars, if you are able to count them, and He said to him, so shall your descendants be.'"* According to many scholars, the real meaning of the Zodiac was displayed to him at that moment, giving credence as to why he was totally able to trust God from that moment on.

Genesis 15:6 speaks of Abram as BELIEVING Him.... *"Abram believed the LORD, and he reckoned it to Him as righteousness"* The word "BELIEVE" here means an <u>unqualified committal of himself, and all that he was or ever would be to God</u>. Another meaning is that he "gave himself up wholly." Abram was able to see that the Promised Messiah would come from a virgin [Virgo], and saw the whole story unfold before him. It began with the virgin and ended with the Lion of Judah [Leo], who would take the keys of the Kingdom from the devil and bring all authority back to God.

A very good book to read on this subject is "The Real Meaning of the Zodiac" by Dr. D. James Kennedy. In this book, Dr. Kennedy spells out the real meaning of the entire zodiac as Abram would have seen it. Abram was able to see in the galaxies God's Plan "B" theme, which made him believe so wholly and where he became totally committed to God. As you study Dr. Kennedy's book, the revelation of the real meaning of the zodiac will become a reality to you as well! Incredibly, satan has tried to keep this meaning a secret for centuries.

— THE REAL MEANING OF THE ZODIAC —

Let us look at what the <u>real</u> zodiac displays:

1. VIRGO = The VIRGIN: She holds the BRANCH, who is JESUS – *Zechariah 6:12; "Then say to him, 'Thus says the LORD of hosts, "Behold, a man whose name is Branch, for He will branch out from where He is; and He will build the temple of the LORD."*
   Isaiah 4:2, "In that day the Branch of the LORD will be beautiful and glorious, and the fruit of the earth will be the pride and the adornment of the survivors of Israel."
2. LIBRA = The SCALES: *Daniel 5:27, "You have-been weighed on the scales and found deficient [wanting]."*
   Psalm 106:10, "So He saved them from the hand of the one who hated them; and redeemed them from the hand of the enemy." That's us! Jesus is our Redeemer, Who purchased us with His Blood!
3. SCORPIO = The SCORPION: *Revelation 12:9, "And the great dragon was thrown down, the serpent of old who is called the devil and satan, who deceives the whole world; he was thrown down to the earth, and his angels were thrown down with him."*

4. SAGITTARIUS = The ARCHER: He is part man and part horse. The victorious, risen and conquering King. He is CHRIST conquering satan. *Revelation 6:1-2 "Then I saw when the Lamb broke one of the seven seals, and I heard one of the four living creatures saying as with a voice of thunder,"Come." I looked, and behold, a white horse, and he who sat on it had a bow; and a crown was given to him, and he went out conquering and to conquer."*

5. CAPRICORNUS = The GOAT: The front half is a GOAT. The rear half is a FISH. The GOAT is in a fallen position, with one leg doubled under his body; the head is bent forward, and he is in a dying situation. However, the TAIL is vigorous and living. This is a beautiful picture of what Christ accomplished by His death.

   Jesus is the SIN OFFERING GOAT, Whose blood was sprinkled on the Mercy Seat. He is both the Lamb of God and the SCAPEGOAT. O.T. Example: *Leviticus 16:20-22, "When he finishes atoning for the holy place and the tent of meeting and the altar, he shall offer the live goat. Then Aaron shall lay both of his hands on the head of the live goat, and confess over it all the iniquities of the sons of Israel and all their transgressions in regard to all their sins; and he shall lay them on the head of the goat and send it away into the wilderness by the hand of a man who stands in readiness. The goat shall bear on itself all their iniquities to a solitary land; and he shall release the goat in the wilderness."* Jesus became our scapegoat on the Cross.

6. AQUARIUS = The WATER-POURER: "POURING FORTH WATER" - *John 7:37-39, "Now on the last day, the great day of the feast, Jesus stood and cried out, saying, If anyone is thirsty, let him come to Me*

and drink. He who believes in Me, as the Scripture said, 'From his innermost being will flow rivers of living water.' But this He spoke of the Spirit, whom those who believed in Him were to receive; for the Spirit was not yet given, because Jesus was not yet glorified." Jesus brings us the water of life.

7. PISCES = The FISHES: These are a representation of the church. *Mark 1:17, "And Jesus said, Follow me and I will make you become fishers of men."*

8. ARIES = The LAMB: Who is this One Who is worthy? JESUS, our Redeemer! *Revelation 5:12 "Worthy is the Lamb that was slain."*

9. TAURUS = The BULL: This is a picture of the coming destruction of the wicked, as Christ comes forth in judgment. Here we see the Lamb changing into the Bull, giving rise to the Christ, who is coming in great glory and in judgment. *II Thessalonians 1:5-8, "This is a plain indication of God's righteous judgment so that you will be considered worthy of the kingdom of God, for which indeed you are suffering. For after all it is ONLY just for God to repay with affliction those who afflict you, and to give relief to you who are afflicted and to us as well when the Lord Jesus will be revealed from Heaven with His mighty angels in flaming fire, dealing out retribution to those who do not know God and to those who do not obey the Gospel of our Lord Jesus."*

10. GEMINI = The TWINS: This Scripture in *Acts 28:11* is a reference to Gemini, the Twins. Two youthful figures are seated side by side and at rest. One has a club resting on his shoulder, and the other one has a harp in one hand, and a bow and arrow in the other. The two bright stars in the heads of these figures represent the mighty warriors, who are now resting joyfully. *"At the end of three months we set sail on an*

Alexandrian ship which had wintered at the island, and which had the Twin Brothers as its figurehead."

11. CANCER = The CRAB: The crab has two claws. He is grabbing something and holding on firmly – the church – held as a possession of Christ – taken to its Heavenly home. (This sounds confusing, and is explained in greater detail in Dr, Kennedy's book.) As the crab lives in two elements, the water and land, so the church lives in two elements, earth and Heaven. The crab's many legs represent the church multiplying. *I Peter 1:3-5, "Blessed be the God and Father of our Lord Jesus Christ! Who according to his great mercy has caused us to be born again to a living hope through the resurrection of Jesus Christ from the dead, to obtain an inheritance which is imperishable and undefiled, and will not fade away, reserved in Heaven for you, who are protected by the power of God through faith for a salvation ready to be revealed in the last time."*

12. LEO = The LION of JUDAH: JESUS! *Revelation 5:5, "Stop weeping; behold, the Lion that is from the tribe of Judah, the Root of David, has overcome so as to open the book and its seven seals."*

The REAL meaning of the Zodiac brings us life everlasting and true GODLY guidance. Satan has and is still working hard to turn this beautiful story into what many use as their own "Horoscope," in order that any credence to the scriptural meaning is totally diminished. Many Christians have no clue that in actual fact there is a real meaning to the "Zodiac" that was laid out by God. Satan has done everything possible to keep this information from God's people.

Chapter Sixteen

— GOD CHANGES THE NAMES
OF ABRAM AND SARAI —

As a result of Abram's trust in what God had shown him, followed by his total unqualified commitment to God, *Genesis 17* states that God changes his name, which was "Abram" (exalted father), to ABRAHAM - the "FATHER OF MANY NATIONS."

In *Genesis 17:4-5,* He says, *"As for me, behold my covenant is with you, and you shall be the father of a multitude of nations. No longer shall your name be called Abram, but your name shall be Abraham, for I will make you the father of a multitude of nations."* Then in *Verse 15-16*, Scripture tells us that, *"God also said to Abraham, 'As for Sarai your wife, you shall not call her name Sarai; but Sarah shall be her name. And I will bless her, and indeed I will give you a son by her. Then I will bless her, and she shall be a mother of nations, kings of peoples shall come from her.'"*

So, God changed her name from "Sarai" (my princess – meaning the princess of her household or tribe), to SARAH – "PRINCESS – the MOTHER OF MANY NATIONS." After that – God performed a miracle – at the age of 90, in spite of her being in her "winter" years, Sarah had Isaac, which means "laughter." Satan was unable to stop God's plan of beginning a pure bloodline after all.

— A GLIMPSE AT SATAN'S QUEST —

In the preceding chapters, we have seen a glimpse of how satan had tried his best to keep God's Plan "B" from reaching total fruition. Amazingly, as we focus in on satan's tactics throughout the Bible – we definitely can see his determination to fight to the end. Satan tried to corrupt every possible blood line to keep the Messiah from becoming a reality. On the other hand, we also see that God is always a few steps ahead of him.

In one sense, we can understand satan's willpower to pursue his quest. After all, he KNOWS where he will be spending eternity. There is NOTHING he can do to change that. The ONLY alternative for him is to retaliate against God by doing whatever it takes to keep mankind out of Heaven and into that "Lake of Fire" with him.

Chapter Seventeen

— A TRIP THROUGH ALL
66 BOOKS OF THE BIBLE —

GENESIS
The First Book of the Pentateuch written by Moses
The "Pentateuch" is referred to as "The Torah" by the
Hebrews
— HOW CHRIST IS BROUGHT TO LIGHT
AND HOW SATAN PURSUES HIS QUEST —

The Book of Genesis: In Genesis, which means "begin-
nings," we see that the pre-existent Christ was very
much involved in the creation. *"In the beginning was the
Word, and the Word was with God, and the Word was God.
He was in the beginning with God. All things came into being
by Him, and apart from Him nothing came into being that
has come into being." John 1:1-3.*

Genesis begins the great salvation story of God's purpose
and plan for His creation. Moses is the human author of
Genesis.

Jesus ministry is anticipated in *Genesis 3:15*, which suggests that the "Seed" of the woman, Who will bruise the serpent's head, is Jesus Christ.

The greatest disclosure of Christ in Genesis is uncovered in God's establishment of His covenant with Abraham in *Genesis 15 and 17*. God made glorious promises to Abraham, and Jesus is the major completion of those promises, a truth explained in detail by Paul in *Galatians 3-5*.

Galatians 3:6-9 tells us, "Even so Abraham believed God and it was reckoned to him as righteousness. Therefore, be sure that it is those who are of faith who are sons of Abraham. The Scripture, foreseeing that God would justify the Gentiles by faith, preached the Gospel beforehand to Abraham, saying, 'All the nations shall be blessed in you, So then those who are of faith are blessed with Abraham, the believer.'"

Abraham's willingness to sacrifice his ONLY son, Isaac in *Genesis 22* is a "type" of God's willingness to sacrifice His ONLY Son, Jesus, for the sins of the world. A type is a symbol, or an object lesson. Types can be found in a person, in a religious ritual, even in a historical event.

EXODUS
The Second Book of the Pentateuch written by Moses
While in Egypt
— THE CHILDREN OF ISRAEL GREW FROM 70 TO OVER TWO MILLION —

The Book of Exodus: This book of Exodus continues the promises that began in the Book of Genesis. From the people of the world, God selected one man, Abraham, and promised to make his descendants into a great nation. Exodus describes the birth of that nation. At the beginning of Exodus we see Jacob, who was called Israel, and his descendants, who were called Hebrews, or (The Children of Israel), going into Egypt and becoming slaves under the Pharaoh.

In *Genesis 37* we read that Jacob's son, Joseph, at the age of 17, was disliked by his 10 older brothers who sold him to Egyptian slave traders. They then lied to their father, stating an animal had killed him. While Jacob was a slave to Pharaoh, he gained the Pharaoh's trust. This occurred after Joseph interpreted a dream that the Pharaoh had. This dream was a warning that there would be a seven year drought following seven years of prosperity. This drought was to be so devastating that the seven year prosperity period would be forgotten. In order for them to survive, Joseph suggested the Pharaoh find a wise man and place him in charge of a nationwide program. His proposal was to collect one fifth of the crops and store it so as to provide the people with food during the upcoming seven lean years.

Since Joseph was the one who was able to interpret the Pharaoh's dream, he was designated to be that overseer. Egypt experienced seven years of affluence, but then, when the second seven years of drought proved to become fatalistic, Egypt was able to provide grain to those in need.

During those years of drought, word got out that there was grain for purchase in Egypt. Jacob sent ten of his sons to Egypt for food. It was during this time that they found Joseph, their very own brother, as the administrator of all distributions. Once reunited, Joseph spoke to the Pharaoh who was filled with compassion and recommended that he invite his family to move to Goshen where they would be taken care of, as it was the best watered and fertile land in the western delta of the Nile River. *Genesis 46:26* tells us that approximately 70 members of Joseph's family came to Egypt. This included his father Jacob, and his eleven brothers, plus their families.

The time came when Jacob, who was called "Israel," died. Joseph and his sons took his body to the land of Canaan and buried him. At the age of 110, Joseph died, yet, in spite of this, the Children of Israel stayed in the land of Goshen.

There came a time when the Pharaoh who loved Joseph also died. Unfortunately the new Pharaoh, who never knew Joseph, hated the Jews and made slaves out of them. After years of torture, the people prayed for deliverance. While in Egypt, they grew to over two million people over a 430 year period.

God sent Moses, the author of this book, to deliver the Children of Israel from their bondage. This deliverance from Egypt was to be considered the greatest miracle ever in the Old Testament. This miracle of liberation was designated by God to become an annual remembrance within the Jewish nation, known as the "Feast of Passover," the "Feast of Unleavened Bread," and the "Feast of First Fruits."

Once they had crossed the Red Sea, they arrived at Mount Sinai where God gave them the Ten Commandments as well as other Laws. In order to become a nation, they now needed a land of their own.

Being descendants of Abraham, Isaac, and Jacob, the Children of Israel remembered they were to be the recipients of the land God had promised to Abraham. God guided them to this land by providing for them a *portable* worship center with the intent of shaping this people into a great nation, in order to be the source of truth and salvation to the entire world. What they discovered was that God was revealing more and more of Himself to them.

In *Exodus,* we see how satan is doing his best to destroy the Israelites and we watch as they go through oppression in Egypt, under the new Pharaoh, and become slaves for 400 years. However, instead of satan being able to witness their demise – Moses, a Jew, who was raised in the Egyptian culture, was called by God to set the Israelites free from the bondage Pharaoh had inflicted upon them. Moses was the one who helped them cross the Red Sea and took them to a place called Mount Sinai. Therefore, Moses is a "type" of Christ, as he delivers them from bondage.

As time elapsed after setting up camp, the Children of Israel became disgruntled. Again, the enemy tried his best to corrupt them while Moses was up on the mountain, hearing from God, and being given the Ten Commandments. As far as the Children of Israel were concerned, Moses was gone way too long. As a result, they convinced Aaron, Moses' brother, to make an idol for them to worship.

In *Exodus 32* we see Aaron asking them for their gold jewelry, out of which he makes them a golden calf. In *verse 7*, God tells Moses that the people he had brought out of Egypt have corrupted themselves and notified him to get down immediately to stop the chaos. God was at a point of destroying all of the Children of Israel, however, they did repent. Yes, satan loses again!

LEVITICUS
The Third Book of the Pentateuch written by Moses
— HOW CAN AN UNHOLY PEOPLE WORSHIP A HOLY GOD? —

The Book of Leviticus: Leviticus focuses on how to live with God, Who is Holy. The children were to be different from those who were around them. Having been slaves, God dramatically rescued them from the bondage in Egypt. God loved them so very much that He wanted them to have His Law, which is known as "Torah," meaning "instruction." Leviticus shows the precise instructions given on how to build a place where Israelites could worship the God of Abraham, Isaac, and Jacob. In this place, they would find God's Holy Presence dwelling among them. They were to be instructed on how to follow Him, how to love Him, and how to think like Him, in order to become His Holy people.

In the book of Exodus, we see the many sacrifices necessary for the Israelites to overcome the many mishaps they seemed to experience. Notice, it does not take long for God's people to become discontented. We see God's forgiveness of sin over and over and over again. We see the costly consequences of sin, but we also see that forgiveness is not something we can have apart from God and His salvation.

The sacrificial system and the high priest are "types" that picture the work of Christ. The Book of *Hebrews, 4:14-15*, describes Christ as Greater than the High Priests of the Old Testament, *"Since then we have a great high priest who has passed through the Heavens, Jesus, the Son of God, let us hold fast our confession. For we do not have a high priest who cannot sympathize with our weaknesses, but one who has been tempted in all things as we are, yet without sin."* Moses uses the instances of Leviticus as a basis for illustrating Christ's work.

Israel's high priest held the highest official religious office in the nation. The writer of Hebrews sought to show that Christianity also had a High Priest, but One Who was in every way superior to the priests of Judaism. The proof of Christ's ability to understand human weakness sympathetically is found in His own experience of temptation, as He was tempted in all areas that man could be tempted, yet would not yield to any of those temptations and sin.

NUMBERS
The Fourth Book of the Pentateuch written by Moses
— MOSES RECORDS THE TRAGIC STORY OF ISRAEL'S UNBELIEF —

The Book of Numbers: Numbers is believed to have been written between 1450 and 1410 BC by Moses. In it, he records a tragic story of regret. The Book of Numbers is the story of nearly forty years of wilderness wandering by the Israelites. Unfortunately, the first generation that came out of Egypt never was able to experience the Promised Land, except for Joshua and Caleb. Instead, the second generation was privileged to encounter the land of milk and honey. This did not happen until all of the first generation had died off.

Remember, Joshua and Caleb were the only two out of the ten tribe leaders who were sent to scout out the "Promised Land" who came back with the faith that God needed for them to have in order to conquer it. Why? Because without faith to conquer and overcome the obstacles they would face, they would be doomed to failure. God could not chance that. He needed a "faith-filled" people to triumph over the land.

We see the first generation traveling towards the border of the Promised Land, but unfortunately they got side tracked. Though God had promised to make them a great, Godly nation and be there for them at all times, providing for their every need, we become aware of their murmurings and rebellion. Regardless of how much God showed His love for them, performing miracle after miracle, they complained. Beginning with the parting of the Red Sea, God continued to prove Himself faithful by providing for them "Manna from Heaven" that they got to eat on a daily basis.

Not ONLY did He provide food for them out of nowhere, water just happened to flow out of a rock, their shoes never wore out, and not one of them ever got sick the whole time they were in the wilderness for those 40 years. Yet, in spite of all this, satan was able to keep them dissatisfied. Unfortunately, God had no choice but to punish the people.

Christ is pictured in Numbers as the "Provider." The apostle Paul writes, concerning Christ, that He was the spiritual Rock Who followed the Israelites through the wilderness and gave them spiritual drink. *I Corinthians 10:4.* "*...and all drank the same spiritual drink, for they were drinking* *from a spiritual rock, which followed them; and the rock was Christ."* Yahweh is the Rock of His people (*Deuteronomy 32*, Moses' song to Yahweh the Rock). Paul now applies this image to the Christ, the Source of the Living Water, the true Rock that accompanied Israel, guiding their experiences in the desert.

Perhaps the greatest tragedy the Israelites experienced was the punishment of not entering the Promised Land due to their unbelief and grumblings. Remember, only Joshua and Caleb were allowed to enter the Promised Land. They were the ONLY ones who came back after scouting out the land with the faith to know they had the ability to conquer it, and do what God had called for them to do. The penalty now was that Joshua and Caleb would have to wait FORTY YEARS. Not only that, ONLY the NEW generation would be able to enter the Promised Land. All of the first generation was to die in the wilderness. God needed a faithful people who would be obedient to His Word. So, forty years later, with a new generation, He began His venture anew.

DEUTERONOMY
The Fifth Book of the Pentateuch written by Moses
— THE CALL TO ISRAEL ON WHO GOD IS —
— WHAT GOD HAS DONE FOR THEM —

The Book of Deuteronomy: Deuteronomy was believed to be the last book written by Moses before he died (approximately 1410-1405 BC). Moses was not able to go into the Promised Land, but God allowed him to see it from the mountain top, just east of the Jordan River.

In Deuteronomy we witness Moses as the first to prophesy the coming of the Messiah, with whom Jesus ever compared Himself. John, the Apostle declares Jesus as saying in *John 5:46-47, "For if you believed Moses, you would believe Me;*

for he wrote of Me. But if you do not believe his writings, how will you believe My words?"

In this book, Moses reminds the Children of Israel of the fact that THEY were God's chosen people whom God had promised to make into a great nation. Moses expounded that they were to be a great witness to the nations around them because of God's love and wisdom. He also reminded them of their special love relationship with God. In fact, God found them so special He was offering them a land of their own, as well as prosperity and victory in battles. All they had to do was merely obey God and they could have everything they needed.

Moses shared with the Israelites the blessings they would attain by being obedient, but warned them also of the curses they would experience if they chose to not obey (see *Deuteronomy 28*). Jesus often quoted from Deuteronomy. When asked to name the most important commandment, He responded with *Deuteronomy 6:5, "And you shall love the Lord your God with all your heart, and with all your soul and with all your might."*

When confronted with satan at His temptation, Jesus quoted exclusively from *Deuteronomy 6:13 and 16; "You shall fear ONLY the Lord your God; and you shall worship Him, and swear by His name. You shall not follow other gods, any of the gods of the peoples who surround you, for the Lord your God in the midst of you is a jealous God; otherwise the anger of the Lord your God will be kindled against you, and He will wipe you off the face of the earth You shall not put the Lord your God to the test, as you tested Him at Massah."* and *Deuteronomy 10:20, "You shall fear the Lord your God; you shall serve Him and cling to Him, and you shall swear by His name."*

What is noteworthy is that the law was given to the first generation on Mt. Sinai. However, they had since died in the desert (except for Joshua and Caleb), and it was this new generation whom Moses gave his three farewell sermons to at the age of 120, just prior to his death. The appointment of Joshua, as Moses' successor, also took place. Moses did what he could to challenge the people to live their future in faith and obedience, as they review their past.

In his first address (*Deuteronomy 1-4*), Moses looked back over the history of Israel, their unbelief as well as the victories God shaped on their behalf, with a final appeal for them to walk in obedience. Remember, only Joshua and Caleb made it to the Promised Land; all the rest were dead because of their unbelief.

In his second address (*Deuteronomy 5-26*), Moses looked up to God and laid out the Israelites responsibility as God's special covenantal people – they were to represent Him and His ways on the earth. They were to obey Him in things great and small.

In his third address (*Deuteronomy 27-33*), Moses *looked out* to warn the Israelites of the consequences of disobedience:

> *Deuteronomy 30:19-20, "I call Heaven and earth as witnesses today against you, that I have set before you life and death, blessings and cursing; therefore choose life, that both you and your descendents may live, that you may love the LORD your God, that you may obey His voice, and that you may cling to Him, for He is your life and the length of your days."*

Moses encouraged the Israelites to be faithful to God's covenant, receive His intended blessings, and instructed them to renew their covenant once they entered the Promised Land. The Levites were chosen to speak publicly from the top of Mount Ebal about the curses awaiting their disobedience to God's law. From the slopes of Mount Gerizim, which was lush with green foliage, the Levites pronounced the blessings promised to those obeying God's law.

What was of great interest to me is that Mount Ebal, from which the CURSES were declared, is still, to this day, brown and barren. Mount Gerizim, on the other hand, where God had His Levitical Priests proclaim God's BLESSINGS, is luxuriantly arrayed with green foliage, in spite of the fact that they are basically across the road from each other, receiving the same sun, the same rain, and the same air.

How noteworthy that Christ, who was perfectly obedient to the Father, even unto death, quoted this book on obedience to demonstrate His submission to the Father's will during the time of His temptations in *Matthew 4:7*! Where Israel had failed to obey God during their wilderness experience, Jesus succeeded in perfect obedience during His. Israel had been in the wilderness for 40 years – Jesus was in the wilderness for 40 days. (*Deuteronomy 29:5 – Matthew 4:2*)

In Deuteronomy, God asked Israel to put the commands of God on her heart for her own good! In the New Covenant in Christ, God did that work Himself and then placed the law into the hearts of the Believer.

Chapter Eighteen

JOSHUA
An Old Testament "Historical" Book

— JOSHUA LEADS THE CHILDREN OF ISRAEL INTO THE PROMISED LAND —

The Book of Joshua: Disobedience is again detected. God named Joshua their leader before Moses died, and then He gave them all clear instructions as to how to conquer the land that He had promised them. At this point, they were still at the east side of the Jordan River where they were when Deuteronomy ended, ready to enter the land that God had promised them. Joshua, the great military commander, had miraculously led the Children of Israel into the Promised Land, crossing the Jordan River into Jericho.

In the Book of Joshua, we see God reclaiming a portion of the earth. You see, there were pagans living in the land who would not accept Jehovah as the one, true God. So, God helped the Children of Israel to cross the Jordan River and advised them as to how to take possession of the land belonging to these pagans. This land was called Canaan.

The instructions were that the Children of Israel were not to take any of the spoils from Jericho, this FIRST city

– meaning, they were to TITHE off their first fruits. Again, just like in the Garden of Eden, God had ONLY asked ONE thing of them. In this case, they were privileged to take the spoils, or the remains, of <u>every</u> city they conquered, <u>except</u> for <u>one </u>city, Jericho. However, satan determined to intervene again. Of all the people, he chose a willing man, named Achan, who was obviously easily swayed to greed. Achan stole possessions that he found and hid them, defying God by doing what was clearly forbidden.

When it came time to conquer the little town of Ai, Joshua assumed that this was an easy city to defeat, not knowing that there was now SIN IN THE CAMP. Subsequently he only sent a few of the troops to do the job. Unfortunately, most all of them were killed. Joshua, not understanding, questioned God about this conundrum, and was informed that there indeed was "sin in the camp." Though it took a bit, Joshua finally discovered who it was. As a resulting punishment, Achan's <u>entire family</u> ended up being destroyed.

Something to digest here....Imagine, here is an ENTIRE family who had to be destroyed due to ONE MAN who chose to be greedy and steal....<u>someone else's sin</u>! What this tells us is that though <u>we</u> may live a moral life – an ancestor could cause us to have to suffer for what he has done. This is called an "ancestral curse."

We might want to look at this seriously. Walking through the Scriptures, we discover that disobeying God [sinning] ultimately costs the violator a tremendous price. (So also with us today!) There does come a time when our disobedience will catch up with us, and the price is usually a weighty one. You can never get away with disobeying God. Some people think they can. They think that if nobody finds out about it, it won't hurt anything. After all, God is merciful. He's not going to hold it against them, right? And if no one else knows...what's the difference?

What they don't realize is that their own hearts will start giving them problems. Their own hearts will start to condemn them. Everyone else may think they are great. They may be spouting faith talk all over the place, but when they come before God in prayer, they will be filled with doubts and fears, which will ultimately keep their prayers from being answered.

As we can see, satan's ploy is to have us delve into a wrongdoing that will, in due course, be a detriment to us. Yet, it is quite possible that nothing unfavorable will happen for YEARS. *Galatians 6:7 says, "Do not be deceived, God is not mocked; for whatever a man sows, this he will also reap."* In other words, we will reap what we sow. This would probably be a time when some of us would like to pray for a "crop failure."

As time goes by, and though we may have lived a good, moral life for many years, without prior notice, we may find ourselves being attacked. Unfortunately, instead of searching our souls to see if we could possibly be reaping what we had sown in the past, we tend to first blame everyone else, or get mad at God, and wonder why He allowed this dilemma to happen to us. Comparing this to *Romans 7 and 8*, Paul explains that it is imperative that REPENTANCE (turning away from the wrongs we have done) must be at the forefront of our walk with God the Father. Completely turning from sin is what brings us freedom from captivity.

We see Christ in the Book of Joshua in three ways:

- By direct revelation
- By types
- By illuminating aspects of His nature

Joshua 5:13-15, says, "Now it came about when Joshua was by Jericho, that he lifted up his eyes and looked, and behold, a man was standing opposite him with his sword drawn in his hand, and Joshua went to him and said to him, 'Are you for us or for our adversaries?'

And he said, 'No, rather I indeed come now as captain of the host of the Lord.' And Joshua fell on his face to the earth, and bowed down, and said to him, 'What has my lord to say to his servant?'

And the captain of the Lord's host said to Joshua, 'Remove your sandals from your feet, for the place where you are standing is holy.'"

This Scripture shows us that the Triune God appeared to Joshua as the *"commander of the army of the Lord."* By His appearance, Joshua was made aware that God Himself was in charge.

Joshua's task was (as it is ours as well) to not dwell on following the Commander's <u>plans,</u> but to <u>know</u> the Commander. It is imperative that we be on <u>His</u> side, not He on ours.

Joshua himself was a "type" of Christ. To reiterate, a <u>type</u> is a <u>symbol</u>, or an <u>object lesson</u>. Types can be found in a person, in a religious ritual, even in a historical event. His name, meaning "Yahweh Is Salvation," is a Hebrew equivalent to the Greek "Jesus." Joshua led the Israelites into the possession of their promised inheritance, just as Christ leads us into possession of eternal life. Joshua proved himself by not relying on his physical ability or cleverness, but had faith in God's ability to overcome on his behalf. We need to do likewise. Our responsibility is to be obedient and faithful to the covenant of God.

As for the aspects of God's nature, let us look at *Joshua 2:17-21, "The men said to her, "We shall be free from this oath to you which you have made us swear, unless, when we come into the land, you tie this cord of scarlet thread in the window through which you let us down and gather to yourself into the house your father and your mother and your brothers and all your father's household."*

"It shall come about that anyone who goes out of the doors of your house into the street, his blood shall be on his own head, and we shall be free; but anyone who is with you in the house, his blood shall be on our head, if a hand is laid on him. But if you tell this business of ours, then we shall be free from the oath which you have made us swear."

"She said, 'According to your words, so be it.' So she sent them away, and they departed; and she tied the scarlet cord in the window."

When Moses sent the two Israelites to check out the Promised Land, Rahab, the harlot was the one who hid them. As a result, she and her family were promised safety from that moment on – IF – she hung a scarlet cord in her window. That red cord in Rahab's window illustrated Christ's redemptive work on the Cross. You see, the blood-red cloth hanging in the window saved Rahab and her household from death. So, too, Christ shed His blood and hung on the Cross to save us from eternal death.

At the end of his life, Joshua testified of Christ's fulfilled promise…*Joshua 23:14, "Now behold, today I am going the way of all the earth, and you know in all your hearts and in all your souls that not one word of all the good words which the Lord your God spoke concerning you has failed; all have been fulfilled for you, not one of them has failed."* He will do the same for us through Christ, Who is "The Promise." <u>In spite of all that satan may try again and again, it will be to no avail. His demise is imminent and God ultimately wins.</u>

JUDGES
An Old Testament "Historical" Book
— A BOOK OF HEROES AS WELL AS A BOOK OF SIN AND ITS CONSEQUENCES —

<u>The Book of Judges:</u> Judges shows us the type of leaders God raised up after Joshua, and gives the history of oppres-

sions and deliverances during the period of the various Judges. The Judges were not kings, but had power and authority like Joshua had. They were spirit-appointed military leaders who took action when Israel needed to be delivered from foreign oppressors. God had not given Israel a leader after Joshua, but had given Israel the land, and a central place of worship, but no government. God Himself was to be the Head of that Nation. Israel was to obey God's laws in return for God's protection and provision.

This book graphically portrays the character of the Lord in His dealings with the Children of Israel. Because of His righteousness, the Lord punished them for their sin; although, due to His love and mercy, He delivered them in reaction to their remorseful cry of repentance. Judges depicts a cyclical, repetitious, and sinful people rebelling against God.

The cycle, repeated throughout the book of Judges, formed the pattern for Israel's bondage and deliverances. The presence of the enemy was to basically test the obedience of the Israelites to God's commands, but it also taught them the art of warfare. God knew the hardness of their hearts, yet wanted them to realize their errors and get back to living God's way. Throughout the Bible, God is doing all He can to help mankind to understand that obedience is by far the best way.

This is a "type" of a loving God Who sent forth His Son, Jesus Christ, as our Deliverer, in order to redeem us from the bondage of sin and death. This came about as a result of God's Plan "B," after Adam had committed high treason in the Garden of Eden. God will be the One Who will judge the world in righteousness. The Apostle Paul tells us in *Acts 17:31: "...Because He has fixed a day in which He will judge the world in righteousness through a Man whom He has appointed, having furnished proof to all men by raising Him from the dead."* <u>That Man is Jesus!</u>

RUTH
An Old Testament "Historical" Book
— A BOOK OF GRACE IN THE MIDST OF DIFFICULT CIRCUMSTANCES —

The Book of Ruth: Written about 1000 BC, the book of Ruth is a love story and is named after Ruth, a young Moabite woman. Moab was east of the Jordan River.

A famine forced Elimelech and his wife Naomi from their Israelite home to the country of Moab.

Naomi, meaning "Pleasant," with her husband, Elimelech, meaning "God is my King," and their two sons, Mahlon, meaning "sickly or unhealthy," and Chilion, meaning "failing or puny," had moved to Moab from Bethlehem in order to escape the famine. Their names depicted that they were unhealthy when they were born. Moab was a country which had begun to worship idols.

Elimelech died and Naomi was left with her two sons. While in Moab, the two sons married Moabite girls, Orpah and Ruth, which was a drastic step, as it was the Moabites who had mistreated the Israelites while on their way to the Promised Land, and were considered their enemy. For an Israelite to marry a Moabite was unlawful unless she converted to Judaism, which apparently had not happened. This would indicate that they had married out of God's will. Naomi, Ruth's mother-in-law, convinced Ruth to follow the God of Abraham, Isaac, and Jacob, and worship Him as the one true God. Later both of the sons died, and Naomi was left alone with Orpah and Ruth in this strange land. Orpah returned to her parents, but Ruth determined to stay with Naomi and they journeyed to Bethlehem.

It is important to notice that Naomi tried to convince the girls to go back to their own Moabite households as the Jewish law would require them to marry next of kin. Naomi pleaded with them, saying that she was way too old to have more children, and even if she did, would they want to wait until those sons grew up to marry them? Orpah took her up on the advice and returned to her family, but Ruth loved her mother-in-law so much she chose to take the consequences.

Ruth opted to follow Naomi back and declared in *Ruth 1:17, "Where you die I will die, and there I will be buried. May the LORD do to me, and worse, if anything but death parts you and me."* Because of that love and devotion, she ended up being the great-grandmother of David, whose lineage brought forth Jesus Christ, the Messiah. Once in Israel, God led Ruth to a man whose name was Boaz. Boaz points toward the redeeming work of Christ. He became Ruth's kinsman and redeemer. Yes, Ruth, the Moabite actually was considered to be important enough to God for Him to place her in the lineage of Jesus, the Messiah!

— LAND and PROPERTIES in ISRAEL —

Significantly, the Israelites did not drive around town looking for properties for sale. Neither would they find real estate agencies who sold acreage in ancient Israel. Israelites could not buy properties as we think of purchasing land property. When money changed hands regarding land in Israel, they were actually only buying the <u>right to use</u> that land for a certain time period. The legal right to the earth is God's, who transferred the deed to the parcel of ground we call Israel, to Abraham...the first Jew...the called-out Gentile...the man of God.

If someone secured the rights of the land from a poor man, then he understood that he could work the ground while the poor man was gone. The land would become his if this poor man never returned. But, in the event that the poor man found wealth, he could return and buy back the rights of his own land. If a close relative of the poor man went to the city council, on behalf of the poor man and requested the property, paid back the dues *(or balance)* to the man who had bought the rights, then under the law of redemption, it would have been mandatory that he relinquish the property at once. The rights to use the land were usually bargained for in measured time periods of years.

So, in the event of bankruptcy, tragedy, or extenuating circumstances, which caused the rightful owner to vacate the premises, the owner would then transfer his rights to someone who would trade money for those rights to farm the land while he was gone. This system was like leasing land but there were no payments, and no one was ever thrown off their own property.

The title deed was actually transferred to someone else until:

1. The rightful owner who was in the lineage returned, or
2. Until someone came on his behalf to redeem his property.

When Elimelech left, he no doubt planned to return with money enough to redeem his own land for his children. He possibly only sold the rights to the land for ten to twenty years, since Naomi stayed in Moab for ten years. However, when Naomi returned, she was destitute with no possible way to ever redeem their land. Even in the year of Jubilee, since she was a woman with no rightful heir, she could not ever hope to have the property back! ONLY if one of her rich, single male relatives would help her redeem Elimelech's property and raise up children in her son's name, would it ever belong to her again. I doubt she ever entertained that thought even in her wildest imaginings, because Ruth, the daughter-in-law who returned with her was a Moabitess. Ruth might as well have had leprosy. Being a Moabitess was that bad.

— BOAZ ENTERS THE PICTURE —

The blessing is that God must have looked at Ruth's dedication and obviously had a purpose for her. As she gleaned in Boaz's field, Boaz noticed her, and saw that she was a virtuous woman. We see that God intervened and honored both Ruth and Naomi by giving Ruth a man to love and Naomi the financial provision she had lost by becoming a widow. This was a perfect example of how God provides for us when we leave our needs in His hands. Ruth found refuge in Israel's God. Jesus' lineage came through Ruth and Boaz.

In the book of Ruth:

- Naomi is symbolic of <u>Israel</u>:
  1. She is rich.
  2. She goes out of the land, apparently because the famine of the land has ousted her. It had not been their choice to have to leave.
  3. Then, because of the problems Naomi incurred in Moab, she comes back empty into the land of Israel and begins to build her life again.

- Ruth is symbolic of the <u>Church</u>, as
  1. She is the Gentile bride, even so
  2. She is related to Boaz by marriage.

- Boaz is symbolic of <u>Jesus Christ</u>, our Messiah.
- The Nearer Kinsman is symbolic of the <u>Law</u>.
  1. Ruth became the great grandmother of King David, placing her in the line of Messiah.

I and II SAMUEL
"Historical" Books of the Old Testament
— BOOKS OF GREAT BEGINNINGS AND TRAGIC ENDINGS (I SAMUEL) —
— DAVID'S PLIGHT OF SUCCESS AND FAILURES, JUST BEING HUMAN —

The Books of I and II Samuel: The Prophet Samuel authored these books approximately 930 BC. God used Samuel to establish a kingship in Israel, as there was no king at that time. God was the One Who wanted to be their King and provide for their every need. They were fully protected and provided for when they chose to follow His laws. He blessed them by causing their crops to grow in abundance. However, the people rejected God's best and wanted a human king. Reluctantly, He granted their demand.

Therefore, Saul became Israel's first king. Both I and II Samuel speak of satan using Saul to try to get rid of David, Israel's second king. The ancestry of David is of great importance and satan knew it. However, his efforts to remove David from the scene were futile, as his labors never came to fruition. We see later that the Messiah did indeed come through the ancestry of David....again, despite satan's futile attempts to thwart it.

The similarities between Jesus and the boy Samuel are striking.

1. Both were children of a promise. Samuel was promised to Hannah! Jesus, the Messiah was promised to Mary!
2. Both mothers expressed their delight in similar fashion. Then, Hannah prayed and said: *"My heart exults in the Lord; my horn is exalted in the Lord, My mouth speaks boldly against my enemies, because I*

rejoice in Thy salvation." I Samuel 1:1. And <u>Mary</u> said: *"My soul exalts the Lord and my spirit has rejoiced in God my Savior, for He has regard for the humble state of the bondslave; for behold, from this time on all generations will count me blessed." Luke 1:46-48*.

3. Both were dedicated to God in a Temple: <u>Samuel</u> – *I Samuel 1:20-28 – "And it came about in due time, after Hannah had conceived, that she gave birth to a son; and she named him Samuel (meaning, "name of God" or "heard of God), saying, 'Because I have asked him of the Lord.' Then the man Elkanah went up with all his household to offer to the Lord the yearly sacrifice and pay his vow."*

"But Hannah did not go up, for she said to her husband, 'I will not go up until the child is weaned; then I will bring him that he may appear before the Lord and stay there forever.' And Elkanah her husband said to her, 'Do what seems best to you. Remain until you have weaned him; only may the Lord confirm His word.' So the woman remained and nursed her son until she weaned him."

"Now when she had weaned him she took him up with her, with a three-year-old bull and one ephod of flour and a jug of wine, and brought him to the house of the Lord in Shiloh, although the child was young."

"Then they slaughtered the bull, and brought the boy to Eli. And she said, 'Oh my lord! As your soul lives, my lord, I am the woman who stood here beside you, praying to the Lord. For this boy I prayed, and the Lord has given me my petition which I asked of Him.'

'So I have also dedicated him to the Lord; as long as he lives he is dedicated to the Lord.' And he worshiped the Lord there."

I Samuel 2:19, "Now Samuel was ministering before the Lord, as a boy wearing a linen ephod (in the Temple). And his mother would make him a little robe and bring it to him from year to year when she would come up with her husband to offer the yearly sacrifice. Then Eli would bless Elkanah and his wife, Hannah, and say, 'May the Lord give you children from this woman in place of the one she dedicated to the Lord.'"

Hannah promised that her son would be dedicated to a lifelong service unto the Lord and would be a lifelong Nazarite (someone who is consecrated or set apart to God), and Eli blessed her for it.

Jesus – *Luke 2:25-35 – "And behold, there was a man in Jerusalem whose name was Simeon; and this man was righteous and devout, looking for the consolation of Israel; and the Holy Spirit was upon him. And it had been revealed to him by the Holy Spirit that he would not see death before he had seen the Lord's Christ."*

"And he came in the Spirit into the temple, and when the parents brought in the child Jesus, to carry out for Him the custom of the law, then he took Him into his arms, and blessed God, and said, 'Now Lord, Thou dost let Thy bond servant depart in peace, according to Thy word; for my eyes have seen Thy salvation, which Thou hast prepared in the presence of all peoples, a light of Revelation to the Gentiles, and the glory of Thy people Israel.'"

"And His father and mother were amazed at the things which were being said about Him. And Simeon blessed them, and said to Mary, His mother,

> *'Behold, this child is appointed for the fall and rise
> of many in Israel, and for a sign to be opposed – and
> a sword will pierce even your own soul – to the end
> that thoughts from many hearts may be revealed.'"*

4. Both were the bridges of transition from one stage of
the nation's history to another. Samuel held the offices
of Priest and King. Christ is Prophet, Priest, and King.
He will come again as King of Kings. David was the
forerunner of the Root of Jesse, who is Jesus Christ.

I and II KINGS
"Historical" Books of the Old Testament
— STORIES OF EVIL RULERS – RAMPANT IDOLATRY – COMPLACENT POPULACE — — BOTH ISRAEL AND JUDAH END UP IN CAPTIVITY —

<u>I and II Kings</u>: The book of I Kings covers a period of
about 120 years, beginning with the death of King David,
and gives us a glimpse of how Solomon, <u>anointed ruler</u> of the
kingdom of Israel for 40 glorious years, built the first Temple,
but then, took his eyes off the Lord. God warned Solomon to
refrain from becoming vulnerable while surrounded with all
this wealth. Obedience is of the essence.

Losing sight of God is easy when everything is going
well for you. Unfortunately, Solomon fell prey to satan's
tactics and allowed himself to think more highly of himself
than he should. The more success he had, the more wives
he attained. In spite of God warning him to NOT take idol
worshipping wives from other cultures, Solomon defied
Him.

The third time God came to him, He [God] reminded him
of all the warnings Solomon had already defied. At this time,
God had to tell him that He would have to remove the reign

from him. However, God would do it through Solomon's son, Rehoboam.

Both I and II Kings show how the reign of all the rulers ultimately came to an end. We have been given His Word and therefore, can count on God's promise that Christ will reign on the throne of David forever. He is coming as the King of Kings and Lord of Lords. *Revelation 19:16 says, "On his robe and on his thigh he has a name written: KING OF KINGS AND LORD OF LORDS."*

There is great importance in understanding that we need to always keep our hearts and minds pure for God. Solomon had so much wisdom and was entrusted by God to build the Temple as dictated by God. God appeared to Solomon three times — at the beginning, the middle, and the end of his time as king.

- The first time, God said, "Solomon, ask me for something good." Solomon asked for wisdom, and God was pleased.
- The second time, God promised Solomon that if he remained faithful, his kingdom would be secure, but if he abandoned God, he would lose his kingdom.
- The third time, God told Solomon that because he had abandoned God, he would now lose the kingdom.

Interestingly, throughout the Bible, God provides us with an understanding of what the Israelites were given, yet how they continually became disgruntled. The enemy [satan] would never cease his attempts to corrupt the bloodline from which the promised Messiah [Jesus] was to come. Remember, He [Jesus] was to redeem the people from that original sin, which was carried out in the Garden. We need to continually bear in mind that even now, God has made us wonderful promises if we remain faithful to him. As a result, what will we choose? Better yet – Whom will we choose?

I and II CHRONICLES
"Historical" Books of the Old Testament
— SUMMARY OF ISRAEL'S HISTORY AFTER THEIR CAPTIVITY —

I and II Chronicles: I Chronicles was written by Ezra, for the Jewish exiles that had come back to the land of Israel after being held captive in Babylon. His purpose was to remind them that they were still God's chosen people. They were helped by understanding God's covenant promises still had meaning for them. These books show the Israelite's genealogy all the way back to Adam, as well as chronicling the happenings from Saul's reign to the "Fall of Jerusalem." Included is the episode when God asks Solomon to build the Temple on Mount Moriah, the very place where He had tested Abraham, and found him faithful. His reward for Abraham being willing to sacrifice Isaac was a ram in the thicket that replaced his son.

I Chronicles narrates the "royal" line of David, which eventually leads to the absolute royalty of Jesus Christ. 2 Chronicles records the history of the Southern Kingdom of Judah, from the reign of Solomon to the conclusion of the Babylonian exile. The deterioration of Judah was definitely disappointing, but the emphasis is given to the spiritual reformers who zealously seek to turn the people back to God.

Christ is foreshadowed in much the same way as He was in I and II Kings. Throughout these Books of the Bible, we see where strife, disobedience and rivalry run rampant. Yet, we see that though satan's strategies may have slowed down progress, he never quite succeeded in accomplishing his line of attack.

EZRA
"Historical" Book of the Old Testament
— EZRA – A PRIEST – SCRIBE –
AND GREAT LEADER —

The Book of Ezra: Satan initiates much strife and turbulence throughout this book, but God always intervened.

• When the people became discouraged due to the enemies' mockings, God faithfully raised up Haggai and Zechariah to encourage the people to complete the task.
• When the people wandered from the truths of God's word, He faithfully sent a devout priest. This priest artfully instructed the people in truth, calling them to confession of sin and repentance from their evil ways.

Throughout the Bible, God comes on the scene whenever satan attempts his schemes. God has always kept His promises. Though God comes to help, the people still need to adjust their lifestyles to be in line with His Word.

God will not and cannot be a puppeteer. He will not allow us to be puppets or robots either. God requires us to use our free choice. We see in Ezra that our sorrows of yesterday can become our successes of today.

Christ is revealed in Ezra by the life he lived and the roles he fulfilled. Ezra represented Christ in that he was one who enthusiastically obeyed the Father. He foreshadowed Christ's role as the "Great High Priest," and finally, Ezra reshaped Israel's spiritual viewpoint, which included a drawing away from dead traditionalism and moral impurity.

NEHEMIAH
"Historical" Book of the Old Testament
— A MAN WHO SAW A PROBLEM AND TOOK ACTION —

In Nehemiah: In this last book written "chronologically," we see him as the associate of Ezra, who called on the people of God to remember God's law. Nehemiah typifies Jesus Christ by the life he modeled, being a courageous leader who defied the odds and encouraged the people to do God's work.

Though Nehemiah saw a problem and was distressed, he did not complain, or wallow in self-pity or grief, but decided to do something about it. Knowing that God wanted him to rebuild the walls in Jerusalem that had been in bad condition, he motivated the people to get involved. From the moment he arrived in Jerusalem, everyone knew who was in charge. He organized, managed, supervised, encouraged the people, and got results. He was a man of action.

Now, satan was not about to pass up the opportunity of creating havoc through constant opposition in trying to dissuade Nehemiah. Yet, in spite of the enemy's tactics, Nehemiah overcame the adversary with prayer, encouragement, guard duty, and consolidation.

So, satan seeing that he was not winning, switched to another scheme, that of an "internal faction." Nevertheless, Nehemiah stood firm and the walls were completely refurbished within 52 days, to the point that everyone knew God was the One Who had helped in this venture. This led to a reaffirmation of faith and revival as the people promised to serve God faithfully. As a result, the book ends with the purging of sin from the land.

Watching Nehemiah in action, we have to search our hearts and ask ourselves if we are or could be someone whom God can count on at a crucial time of need. In other words, will we take authority over the enemy, or cower and give up?

ESTHER
"Historical" Book of the Old Testament
— A LADY WHO TOOK ACTION AND PRESERVED GOD'S PEOPLE —

The Book of Esther: In this book there is intrigue, danger, and deliverance. The beat goes on. The setting was the Persian Empire, approximately 483 - 473 BC. Though in captivity, far from the promise land, this story shows how God cared for His people in order to keep His promise to bring them back to their homeland. Though the name of God is not mentioned in Esther, you can see God's providential hand as surely as in any other book in the Bible. Satan's plot was to use Haman in order to destroy the entire Jewish people.

This book begins with Queen Vashti of Persia refusing to obey an order from her husband, King Xerxes, who happened to be drunk when he gave that order. By doing so, she faced the consequence of being forever banished from her husband's presence, based on the cultural law of Persia. As a result, King Xerxes sent out a decree, asking for all the beautiful women in the empire to come to the royal harem so he could find a wife to replace the Queen.

Esther, a beautiful young Jewish girl, living in exile with her people in Persia, was one of those chosen. Esther had been an orphan, and was considered a "nobody" in that culture. She was being raised by her older cousin, Mordecai. Mordecai, who happened to become one of the government officials for King Xerxes, stayed near the palace and kept a close watch to make sure she stayed safe. Esther ultimately became Queen.

One day while on duty at the palace, Mordecai over-heard two of the King's eunuchs planning to assassinate King Xerxes. Upon hearing that, he gave the information to Queen Esther, who told the King, giving Mordecai full credit for saving the King's life. As a result, both eunuchs were hanged by the gallows.

As time went by, the King promoted Haman to be his second-in-command officer. Everyone was expected to bow to Haman as a sign of respect, whenever he [Haman] would pass by. However, Mordecai refused, as he considered the God of Abraham, Isaac, and Jacob, the ONLY one he would ever bow in respect for. Consequently, Haman found Mordecai a "thorn in his side," hating him, even though Mordecai tried, in vain, to explain to him his devotion to His "Jewish" God.

Haman, filled with rage at Mordecai's so-called disrespect, determined to get rid of him. However, he [Haman] decided that he would not bother eliminating just Mordecai, but would exterminate the entire Jewish population, as, in his own mind, all "pious" Jews would refuse to bow before a mere man. Another strategy of satan! He just happened to find a man with a hardened heart in Haman who was willing to fulfill this mission.

Haman convinced King Xerxes that there were people amongst them who went against protocol by not obeying the King's decree, which stated that all were to respect Haman's position by bowing as he passed by them. Interestingly, he never mentioned to King Xerxes that they were Jews. He offered to pay 10,000 talents out of his own pocket to the administrators who would exterminate the "culprits." Because the King trusted Haman, he used his signet ring on the letters that went out to all the kings and provinces, approving this venture.

In conclusion, Mordecai heard about this plot, and was able to convince Esther to be willing to sacrifice her own life in order to protect God's chosen people by insisting that she notify King Xerxes of Haman's scheme. Since it was the custom for a queen to never enter the king's domain unless He called for her, she was risking her life by initiating the move towards him. God intervened and she remained unharmed.

In the end, King Xerxes listened to Esther's plea to revoke the decree and explained Haman's tactics. Thus, Haman was hanged on the gallows, which he had prepared for Mordecai. King Xerxes replaced Haman with Mordecai as his right hand man. The estate of Haman went to Queen Esther, and another letter went out immediately reversing the edict so all the Jews were spared from annihilation and guaranteed protection throughout the land.

To celebrate this historic occasion, the Festival of Purim was established. In fact, the Jewish people still celebrate this story annually during the Jewish Feast of Purim. Again, satan's strategy failed! I would encourage you to read the entire book of Esther, and experience this incredible story of love, devotion, and dedication.

Queen Esther was similar to Jesus through her submission, dependence, and obedience to her God-given authorities. Like Jesus, she fasted and prayed for her people. Finally, Esther was willing to give up her life in order to save the nation from certain death. For this, she was exalted by the king.

In like fashion, Jesus gave up His life that a world of sinners, as a result of Adam's sedition, might be saved from eternal death. For this, Jesus was highly exalted by God. Paul explains it this way in *Philippians 2:5-11, "Have this attitude in yourselves, which was also in Christ Jesus, who, although He existed in the form of God, did not regard equality with God a thing to be grasped, but emptied Himself, taking the form of a bond-servant and being made in the likeness of men. And being found in appearance as a man, He humbled*

Himself by becoming obedient to the point of death, even death on a cross. Therefore also God highly exalted Him, and bestowed on Him the name which is above every name, that at the name of Jesus every knee should bow, of those who are in Heaven, and on earth, and under the earth, and that every tongue should confess that Jesus Christ is Lord, to the glory of God the Father."

Chapter Nineteen

JOB
A "Poetic" Book of the Old Testament

— A GRIPPING DRAMA of GOING FROM RICHES to RAGS to RICHES —

The Book of Job: This tells the story of Job, the man seen as a "type" of Christ, as he was clearly considered a blameless man, yet suffered greatly. Job was a prosperous farmer living in the land of Uz. He had thousands of sheep, cattle, and other livestock, a large family, and many servants. Satan came before God claiming that Job trusted God and everything was going well with him only because of his riches. *Job 1:6-10, "Now there was a day when the sons of God came to present themselves before the LORD, and satan also came among them. The LORD said to satan, 'From where do you come?' Then satan answered the LORD and said, 'From roaming about on the earth and walking around on it.'"*

"The LORD said to satan, 'Have you considered My servant Job? For there is no one like him on the earth, a blameless and upright man, fearing God and turning away

from evil.' Then satan answered the LORD, 'Does Job fear God for nothing? Have You not made a hedge about him and his house and all that he has, on every side? You have blessed the work of his hands, and his possessions have increased in the land.'"

Consequently, Job was humbled and stripped of everything he had. To make matters worse, his body was covered with painful sores. What is most interesting in the story of Job is that not only does satan attack Job physically, but uses Job's own wife to try to get him to turn his back on his God and reject Him. His wife told him to curse God.

His three closest friends tried to convince him that he must have sinned to cause such demise in his life, and needed to confess his sins, repent, and turn back to God. But, Job maintained his innocence and in the end his wealth was restored twice as much as he had lost, he was healed, and he then became the intercessor for his friends. Through all of this we see that God is sovereign and just in all His ways, even when we do not know or cannot understand His purposes.

Paralleled to Job, Christ suffered, was persecuted for a time by men and demons, felt forsaken by God, and then became an intercessor. I would highly recommend reading a book by Philip Yancey, someone who had a "Job like" experience, and who tells how he conquered his dilemma. The book is called *"Prayer, Does It Make Any Difference?"*

PSALMS
A "Poetic" Book of the Old Testament
— HONEST FEELINGS EXPRESSED FROM DESPAIR TO JUBILATION —

The Book of Psalms: Psalms opens one's heart to God. It is considered the hymnbook and prayer book of the Bible. Some of the Psalms date back to Moses while others were written after the return from exile. Approximately half of these Psalms were written by David. The Book of Psalms is filled with Prophetic statements about the Messiah and Who He was to be. Remember that "hind sight is 20/20 vision." When these predictions were made – nothing was in place to prove what the Prophets of Old had revealed.

Now, in looking back, everything comes into position. Take for instance:

- *Psalm 22:1, "My God, my God, why hast thou forsaken me?"* This was a prophecy of Jesus on the Cross.
- *Psalm 22:6, "But I am a worm* (this was a crocus worm. If they crushed it, then purple dip would come out of it), *and not a man, a reproach of men, and despised by the people."* He was scorned on the Cross.
- *Psalm 22:4-5, "In You our fathers trusted; They trusted and You delivered them. To You they cried out and were delivered; In You they trusted and were not disappointed."* Jesus also still trusted the Word and freely quoted it, even when He couldn't trust the people.
- *Psalm 22:12-13, "Many bulls have surrounded me; strong bulls of Bashan have encircled me. They open wide their mouth at me, as a ravening and roaring lion."* Bulls like new things and will surround, then attack their prey. In Jesus' case, there were a lot of bulls.
- *Psalm 22:14, "I am poured out like water, and all my bones are out of joint. My heart is like wax; it is melted within me."* Jesus was totally unrecognizable as a human being after having endured the flaying He received from the soldiers, scribes, and Pharisees [bulls].

117

- *Psalm 22:15, "My strength is dried up like a potsherd* [sun-baked clay], *and my tongue cleaves to my jaws;"* He was thirsty on the Cross. *"Thou dost lay me in the dust of death.*
- *Psalm 22:16, "For dogs have surrounded me; a band of evil doers have encompassed me, they pierced my hands and my feet."* Not ONLY did spikes go through His hand, and feet, but the soldiers [bulls] also pierced His side.
- *Psalm 22:17, "I can count all my bones; they look, they stare at me.*
- *Psalm 22:18, "They divide my garments among them and for my clothing they cast lots."* At the foot of the cross they cast lots for His clothes.
- *Psalm 22:19, "But Thou, O Lord, be not far off; O Thou my help, hasten to my assistance.*
- *Psalm 22:20-21, "Deliver my soul from the sword, my only life from the power of the dogs. "Save me from the lion's mouth* [satan's cohorts]; *and from the horns of the wild oxen Thou dost answer me."* However, Jesus did get the keys from satan after He paid that incredibly painful price for us. He had the sin "ON" Him, but never "IN" Him.

He even took some with Him as we see in *Matthew 27:50-53, "And Jesus cried out again with a loud voice, and yielded up His spirit. And behold, the veil of the temple was torn in two from top to bottom, and the earth shook; and the rocks were split, and the tombs were opened; and many bodies of the saints who had fallen asleep were raised; and coming out of the tombs after His resurrection they entered the holy city and appeared to many."* These bodies were the Old Testament Saints of God who believed in the coming Redeemer.

Now comes the victory cry: *Psalm 22:22-25, "I will tell of Thy name to my brethren; in the midst of the assembly I will praise Thee. You who fear the Lord, praise Him; all you descendants of Jacob, glorify Him, and stand in awe of Him, all you descendants of Israel. For He has not despised nor abhorred the affliction of the afflicted; neither has He hidden His face from him; but when he cried to Him for help, He heard. From Thee comes my praise in the great assembly; I shall pay my vows before those who dear Him."*

Psalm 22:26-31, "The afflicted shall eat and be satisfied; those who seek Him will praise the Lord. Let your heart live forever! All the ends of the earth will remember and turn to the Lord, and all the families of the nations will worship before Thee. For the kingdom is the Lord's, and He rules over the nations. All the prosperous of the earth will eat and worship. All those who go down to the dust will bow before Him, even he who cannot keep his soul alive. Posterity will serve Him; it will be told of the Lord to the coming generation. They will come and will declare His righteousness to a people who will be born, that He has performed it."

Bottom line – everyone will bow before the Lord one day, despite their former beliefs or actions, satan included. Let the honesty of the Psalms lead us all into a deeper relationship with God.

PROVERBS
"Poetic" Books of the Old Testament
— THE DIFFERENCE BETWEEN KNOWLEDGE AND WISDOM —

The Book of Proverbs: Knowledge is good, but there is quite a difference between having facts [knowledge] and taking those facts and applying them to life [wisdom]. Without wisdom, our knowledge is useless. Solomon gave us insight as to how to use wisdom to live out what knowledge we have. Solomon, the author of Proverbs, Ecclesiastes, and Song of Solomon, gives practical insights and guidelines on how to live our lives.

The main theme of Proverbs is the nature of true wisdom. Solomon writes, *"The fear of the Lord is the beginning of knowledge. Only fools despise wisdom and discipline" (Proverbs 1:7).* He then proceeds to give hundreds of examples on how to live according to godly wisdom. Those who learn this awesome respect for God can become wise in His ways.

As you read Proverbs, you hear Solomon point out that knowing God is the "Key to Wisdom." As you listen with your heart to the lessons Solomon lays out, and begin to put these into action, you will discover that the revelation that comes to you will solidify your understanding of Who God is. You will also begin to comprehend more and more what it meant for Him to sacrifice His only Son in order that what was begun with Adam's disloyalty could indeed be eradicated.

Remember, all the wisdom and the Prophetic words of old lead us to the knowledge and understanding that Jesus had to become the "Ultimate Blood Sacrifice" in order for us to have access into God's domain.

The Bible is filled with information on what the Children of Israel did out of obedience to God's Word and the blessings they experienced as a result. However, it also allows us to catch sight of the trials and tribulations they had to overcome. And finally, we catch a glimpse of the judgments that came as a result of their disobedience.

ECCLESIASTES
"Poetic" Book of the Old Testament
— NEGATIVE AND PESSIMISTIC, YET THE LAST CHAPTER BRINGS RESOLVE —

The Book of Ecclesiastes: Solomon tells us of the journey of his life which depicts the dilemma in his experience of a most "meaningless" life. Everything he tried, tested, and experienced seemed pointless to him. He felt that life was useless, pointless, irrational, foolish and empty....an exercise in futility.

We have to remember that this came from a man who, in reality, seemed to "have it all." After all, he was considered the "wealthiest" man, not to mention the "wisest." He had intellect, power, and wealth. On the contrary, all of a sudden he became foolish. However, after becoming extremely depressed by the disappointments in life, he finally repented.

After his biographical tour of his life, he gives us insight into his conclusive thoughts. He encourages us in *Ecclesiastes 12:13* to *"Fear God and obey His commands,"* for this is the duty of every person. God will judge us for everything we do, including every secret thing, whether it is good or bad. Solomon ends up warning us that apart from a right relationship with God, life is futile. We are urged to fear God and to obey His commandments, while enjoying life to the fullest, and to remember that this is a gift from God, provided through God's Plan "B."

Although the tone of Ecclesiastes is negative and pessimistic, the entire book is filled with wisdom on how to overcome adversities. All of his remarks, due to the futility of life, are there for a purpose and are of great value to us. The main purpose is to help us seek fulfillment and happiness in God alone. His purpose was not to destroy all hope, but for us to realize our hope is in God alone, Who has purposed to go through the most devastating sacrifice.

Let us imagine now going through life knowing that we would never have a relationship with God ever again and that our destination would indeed be the "Lake of Fire." In going back to the beginning of this writing, we can see how our lives would have become without God. We have the <u>free choice </u>to either have a relationship with God or to ignore Him. For those of us who have been on both sides, we know, without a doubt, that life on the side of God is far more rewarding, peaceful, and hopeful. Without Him, life would definitely be futile.

So – would it not be of the essence for us to thank God that He had gone to Plan "B" in order that we can attain that hope of eternal bliss with Him throughout eternity? If suicide bombers would have had the knowledge and understanding that God has provided an opportunity for each of them to live with Him in love and peace forever in Heaven, then imagine how many lives there could have been spared. One could only believe that they would have chosen the other route…God's route.

SONG OF SOLOMON
"Poetic" Book of the Old Testament
— A DIALOGUE OF INTIMACY —

<u>Song of Solomon</u>: Solomon brings us into an exquisite charm and beauty of love as one of God's incredibly wonderful gifts to us. This book tells the romantic story of Solomon and his bride, from their first meeting and courtship and then finally, their marriage, which points out that this kind of love is worth waiting for. The entire Book reminds us of God's love and passion for His people [Bride], and of Jesus Christ's self-sacrificing love for His church.

Chapter Twenty

— THE BOOKS OF THE "MAJOR" PROPHETS —

The following books in the Old Testament are called the Prophetic Books. Each book is about the works of God's Prophets. In the years that the kings ruled in the Jewish Kingdoms of Israel in the North and to Judah in the South, God spoke through the Prophets. Isaiah the Prophet, as well as the other Prophets to follow, served as the conscience of the people, calling them to repent and turn from their ungodly ways, and then to obey and trust in God Almighty.

ISAIAH
Old Testament "Major Prophet" Book
— A STRONG AND COURAGEOUS PROPHET WHO SPOKE FOR GOD —

Isaiah: Isaiah was the most eloquent of the Prophets, and the one whom God chose to analyze the failures of those nations around him. It was Isaiah who pointed to the Promised Messiah Who would bring peace. Isaiah speaks of the Messiah more than any other Prophetic book in the Old Testament. Isaiah resided in Jerusalem during the time of the tempestuous development of the Assyrian Empire towards the end of BC.

Isaiah is the one who helps us to more clearly understand God's full <u>judgment</u> due to the sins of God's chosen people. By the same token, he also unveils the full judgment of God's <u>salvation</u>. Isaiah is the one who gives us insight into the time when the Lord's Kingdom will be on earth, during which the Messiah becomes the Righteous Ruler. He also prophesies of Christ's death on the Cross for the redemption of mankind as *"The Suffering Servant."*

In verses 1-3 – He became our "Meal Offering!"

- *Isaiah 53:1, "Who has believed our message? And to whom has the arm of the LORD been revealed?"* It is Jesus who is the arm of the Lord!
- *Isaiah 53:2, "For He grew up before Him like a tender shoot, and like a root out of parched ground; He has no stately form or majesty that we should look upon Him, nor appearance that we should be attracted to Him."* By the time the scribes and Pharisees got through with Him, His body was unrecognizable.
- *Isaiah 53:3, "He was despised and forsaken of men, a man of sorrows and acquainted with grief; and like one from whom men hide their face He was despised, and we did not esteem Him."* In the original Hebrew, *"makos"* [sorrows] meant <u>pain</u>; *"choli"* [grief] meant <u>sickness</u> or <u>disease</u>. The Messiah bore the consequences of man's original sin, although the Children of Israel did not realize it at the time.

In verses 4-6 – He became our "Peace Offering!"

- *Isaiah 53:4, "Surely* (not perhaps, but surely) *our griefs* [sickness] *He Himself bore, and our sorrows* [pain] *He carried; Yet we ourselves esteemed Him stricken, smitten of God, and afflicted."*
- *Isaiah 53:5, "But He was pierced through for our transgressions, He was crushed for our iniquities; the chastening for our well-being fell upon Him, And by His scourging we are healed* (we ARE healed)."
- *Isaiah 53:6, "All of us like sheep have gone astray, each of us has turned to his own way; but the LORD has caused the iniquity of us all to fall on Him."*

In verse 7 – He became our "Sin Offering!"

- *Isaiah 53:7, "He was oppressed and He was afflicted, yet He did not open His mouth; like a lamb that is led to slaughter, and like a sheep that is silent before its shearers, so He did not open His mouth."*
- *Isaiah 53:8, "By oppression and judgment He was taken away; and as for His generation, who considered that He was cut off out of the land of the living for the transgression of my people, to whom the stroke was due?"* The unjust judicial that Christ was subjected to is revealed in this verse. The Jewish Sanhedrin violated its own laws:
  1. They met at the home of Caiaphas rather than their regular meeting place.
  2. They met at NIGHT rather than during the day.
  3. They convened on the eve of a Sabbath day and a festival.

4. They pronounced judgment on the same day as the trial.
5. They ignored the formalities, which would have allowed the possibility of acquittal, which could happen in capital sentences.

• *Isaiah 53:9, "His grave was assigned with wicked men, yet He was with a rich man in His death, because He had done no violence, nor was there any deceit in His mouth."*

In verse 10 – He became our "Trespass Offering!"

• *Isaiah 53:10, "But the LORD was pleased to crush Him, putting Him to grief; If He would render Himself as a guilt offering, He will see His offspring, He will prolong His days, and the good pleasure of the LORD will prosper in His hand."*
• *Isaiah 53:11, "As a result of the anguish of His soul, He will see it and be satisfied; by His knowledge the Righteous One, My Servant, will justify the many, as He will bear their iniquities."*
• *Isaiah 53:12, "Therefore, I will allot Him a portion with the great, and He will divide the booty with the strong; because He poured out Himself to death, and was numbered with the transgressors; yet He Himself bore the sin of many, and interceded for the transgressors."*

Also see *Matthew 27:*

• *Verse 28, "They stripped Him and put a scarlet robe on Him."*
• *Verse 29, "And after twisting together a crown of thorns, they put it on His head, and a reed in His*

right hand; and they knelt down before Him and mocked Him, saying, 'Hail, King of the Jews!'"
- *Verse 30, "They spat on Him, and took the reed and began to beat Him on the head."*
- *Verse 31, "After they had mocked Him, they took the scarlet robe off Him and put His own garments back on Him, and led Him away to crucify Him."*

JEREMIAH
Old Testament "Major Prophet" Book
— WHO MOST OF HIS LIFE STOOD ALONE – WAS SPECIAL TO GOD —

The Book of Jeremiah: Jeremiah, the Prophet, ministered in his Prophetic role for almost fifty years and throughout the reign of five kings. He led an emotionally tortured life, yet was able to hold to his strong message, which shows us his emotions and feelings. God used him to warn the Children of Israel of how they must return to obedience and to the God of Abraham, Isaac, and Jacob, or they would face a catastrophe. They were to be God's source of information to the nations. Unfortunately, in spite of Jeremiah's pleas, they did not repent.

Sadly, Jeremiah saw his prediction of their plight come to fruition with the fall of Jerusalem to Nebuchadnezzar, the Babylonian king. He also witnessed the destruction of the Temple, as well as the exile to Babylon for many of the Israelites. The good news is, Jeremiah was able to tell of the return of God's people from exile, as well as the restoration of the nation of Israel. Jeremiah also informed them of the time when the Messiah would come and bring world wide blessing.

LAMENTATIONS
Old Testament "Major Prophet" Book
— WE SEE WHY HE WAS CALLED THE WEEPING PROPHET —

<u>The Book of Lamentations</u>: In this book, Jeremiah conveys the sorrows he felt for the fallen city of Jerusalem. Most believe that he was actually an eye witness to the destruction, which would have been about 586 BC. He wrote about Jerusalem and the burning of the Temple. His words in *Lamentations 1:16, "For these things I weep; my eyes run down with water; because far from me is a comforter, One who restores my soul. My children are desolate because the enemy has prevailed,"* describes the sorrow he felt in watching this happen. He shows his devastation while watching the Children of Israel being escorted to Babylon, hundreds of miles away.

Jeremiah expresses God's sympathy for His people when He sees them suffering with the words from *Lamentations 3:22, "The LORD'S loving kindnesses indeed never cease, His compassions never fail."* Jeremiah brings out the fact that God had no choice but to judge righteously, when His people disobeyed and turned away from Him. This grieved God, because His longing was for them to return to Him.

In time, Jeremiah points out that they would repent, at which point God would keep His promise and bring them back into the fullness of His love, in order that they would indeed be a "Light to the Nations!"

EZEKIEL
Old Testament "Major Prophet" Book
— FEARLESSLY PREACHED ON THE STREETS OF BABYLON —

<u>The Book of Ezekiel</u>: Ezekiel was one of the more than 10,000 Jewish people exiled to Babylon by King Nebuchadnezzar in 597 BC. He was in Babylon while Jeremiah was in Jerusalem. Interestingly, while Jeremiah prophesied the destruction of Jerusalem, Ezekiel, at that same time, was prophesying that the same fate would be for those Israelites who chose to disobey God. In 586 BC, both the city of Jerusalem and the Temple were burned and Israel's line of earthly kings ended.

However, God wanted them to know that all was not in vain and that He was the Lord. He again wanted them to lean on HIM as their King, serving God alone, rather than rely on an earthly king. Ezekiel does bring hope and comfort to the Children of Israel after the fall of Jerusalem, with the Prophetic word that the Messiah will reign from a new Temple in Jerusalem, and that ultimately they WOULD return to their home land. When the years of captivity ended, God brought His people back and restored their covenant relationship. *(Ezekiel 36 and 37)*

DANIEL
Old Testament "Major Prophet" Book
— NEVER GAVE UP OR GAVE IN, BUT HELD FAST TO HIS FAITH —

<u>Daniel</u>: This book is the KEY to understanding Biblical prophesies. In this book, many "End Time" happenings are presented. It is imperative to read the book of Daniel in order to adequately understand other prophecies in the Bible that were written by authors other than Daniel. Daniel, at about

15 years of age, was also among those who had been taken captive to Babylon. This was at the time that the armies of Babylon first came into Jerusalem in approximately 605 BC. Daniel lived under Babylonian and then Persian rule. Because of his integrity, God was able to use Daniel to encourage and show others how to trust God, who controls the universe and all of history. Daniel inspired the Children of Israel to understand that in spite of all they had experienced, God still had a mission and a future for His people.

The Book of Daniel begins with the story of his childhood into manhood. Because Daniel had experienced visions, he was able to prophesy of the rise and fall of several empires, which began with Babylon. He brings to light knowledge of the antichrist who will be reigning during what is called the "The Seven Year Tribulation" period. He also brings the good news of the second coming of the Messiah.

We have seen in many of the Old Testament books the references to the Messiah and who He is. In the book of Daniel, we see Him as the "Conquering King" Who will overthrow the antichrist at the end of the "Seven Year Tribulation." Daniel has a vision of God's Plan "B" where God informs the serpent in *Genesis 3:15* of his demise. *"... I will put enmity between you and the woman, and between your seed and her seed; He shall bruise you on the head, and you shall bruise him on the heel."*

What we are discovering as we go through each book of the Bible is how the message of the coming Messiah has been interwoven throughout. No matter how many years have transpired, God has always chosen and informed His own trusted delegate along the way, in order to <u>never</u> allow this vital message to die.

We need to realize also that there were no such things as newspapers, TVs, or radios. God had to keep His people abreast of His plans of redemption through someone He could trust. Therefore He used dreams and visions to communicate His plans to His designated Prophet. Each Prophet then spoke on behalf of God to the Children of Israel.

Chapter Twenty-One

HOSEA
Old Testament "Minor Prophet" Book

— GOD'S LOVE FOR HIS PEOPLE AND THE RESPONSE FROM HIS BRIDE —

The Book of Hosea: Unlike any other book in the Bible – we see in Hosea how God so lovingly and patiently pursues us. Hosea was described as someone who was betrayed by his bride, yet continues to love her with a passion, regardless of her unfaithfulness. This scenario describes God's loyal love for His own people, Israel, who so many times proved to be unfaithful to Him. God used the story of Hosea as a last loving appeal to try to help the Northern Kingdom to understand His love for them.

There were three names Hosea used to describe the Northern Kingdom:

- Israel, which was the most common
- Ephraim, the most powerful tribe in the North
- Samaria, which was the Capitol of the North

The nation, Israel, had been as unfaithful as a prostitute, continually pursuing pagan gods. Hosea was the last voice of a faithful loving God to the Northern Kingdom before its destruction in 722 BC.

JOEL
Old Testament "Minor Prophet" Book
— CATCH HIS VISION OF GOD'S POWER AND MIGHT —

The Book of Joel: Joel's name means, "The Lord is God!" God's hand of discipline reaches out to restore those He loves. Joel wrote this book about 835 BC. He brings a constant reminder of the "One true God." He illustrates God's discipline with the locusts and the drought, speaking of coming judgments, such as "The Day of the Lord," which had meaning to the Jewish people in his day. God was offering restoration and blessing through His Prophet, Joel, as well as the promise that He will indeed send His Spirit.

AMOS
Old Testament "Minor Prophet" Book
— GOD GAVE A HUMBLE SHEPHERD BOY A VISION TO BE DECLARED —

The Book of Amos: Amos emphasizes, in these nine chapters, the words, "Prepare to Meet Your God!" Amos was not a priest or a king, but a shepherd, living about ten miles south of Jerusalem. This actually was in the Southern Kingdom of Judah. However, God sent him to the Northern Kingdom, called Israel, to announce judgment in approximately 760-755 BC, because the prosperous, socially corrupt Northern Kingdom had broken so many of God's laws, including the law to not worship pagan idols.

Amos, meaning "Burden," carried this very heavy message of judgment from God up to the center of the false worship, in Bethel. However, for those who loved God, Amos brought a word of encouragement...the day would come when the Kingdom of David would be re-established and God's people would dwell in safety.

OBADIAH
Old Testament "Minor Prophet" Book
— GOD'S RESPONSE TO THOSE WHO HARM HIS CHILDREN —

The Book of Obadiah: The book of Obadiah is only one chapter long, yet the prophecy is clear. It centers between Edom and Israel. Edom bordered the land of Israel to the south east. The Edomites were descendants of Esau. They carried a grudge against their relatives in Israel because Esau's twin brother Jacob had cheated Esau out of his birthright.

Edom had a tendency to gloat whenever they heard of Israel's devastations, captured and delivered fugitives to the enemy, and even looted Israel's countryside. Because of this, Obadiah had to warn them of their destruction and that God's Kingdom and God's people would triumph, in spite of them. We see that Edom ultimately disappeared.

JONAH
Old Testament "Minor Prophet" Book
— GOD ASKS HIM TO GO TO THE WORST OF ALL SINNERS —

The Book of Jonah: The book of Jonah shows that God desired the salvation of all people, not just the Jewish people. God had told Jonah to go to Nineveh, Israel's most dreaded enemy, to tell them that God would spare them from destruction if they would repent. But Jonah defied God's request and sailed in the opposite direction as he basically wanted the people of Nineveh to suffer for the misdeeds they had done. This was when God had to intervene and prepare a fish to swallow Jonah and to deliver him to Assyria. In the end – Jonah did deliver the message to Nineveh, and Nineveh turned to God, but Jonah sulked because they were not destroyed.

The story of Jonah shows us God's heart and how He desires to pursue ALL people. Jonah also shows us that the people of Israel were chosen to introduce all nations to God. From the beginning of time, God's intent was to redeem ALL to Him.

MICAH
Old Testament "Minor Prophet" Book
— A PICTURE OF ALMIGHTY GOD WHO HATES SIN, BUT LOVES THE SINNER —

<u>The Book of Micah</u>: The book of Micah summarized much of what the other Prophets had said to their people. He beckoned them in *Micah 6:8*, *"… to act justly and to love mercy, and to walk humbly with your God."* He then warned that God would punish them for their wealth and power and injustice. He brought his message to the common people of the Southern Kingdom. Though he had to warn them, he followed with the message of HOPE of the coming Messiah!

NAHUM
Old Testament "Minor Prophet" Book
— PREDICTS THAT THIS NATION WILL BE TOTALLY DESTROYED —

<u>The Book of Nahum</u>: The Book of Nahum pronounces God's judgment on the Capitol of Assyria, Nineveh. During

Jonah's time, Nineveh repented of her sins and God spared the city. However, about 100 years later, Nineveh reverted to its extreme wickedness, cruelty and pride. Because Assyria crushed the Northern Kingdom, Nahum prophesied Nineveh's fall. The Prophet Nahum shows us that God rules over all the earth and that His righteous standards apply to ALL people.

We continually see God's intent to lead all people to seek HIM in all they do. Remember, satan was out to do all he could to try to prevent the Messiah from being able to appear. He tried it by corrupting the blood lines – he tried by turning people away from God – he tried in about every way possible.

Yes, God is a loving and forgiving God, but He also has to punish those who have made the CHOICE to NOT follow Him. In some cases, He had to literally destroy them. This does not mean that God is cruel, but does mean that He will do what He must to fulfill Plan "B," which was implemented in the Garden of Eden when Adam committed high treason.

HABAKKUK
Old Testament "Minor Prophet" Book
— SHOWS GOD IS STILL IN CONTROL DESPITE TRIUMPH OF EVIL —

The Book of Habakkuk: The book of Habakkuk shows the Prophet addressing GOD, not the people. In this frank dialogue with God, Habakkuk asked two questions that troubled him.

1. Why did God allow wicked people to prosper without being punished? He saw that the leaders of Judah were oppressing the poor.

   God's answer was that Judah would be punished by Babylon.

137

2. After that, Habakkuk asked why God would use a country that was even more sinful to punish His people.

   God explains that Babylon would also be punished once it had accomplished His purpose.

Shortly after this dialogue, we see that Habakkuk trusted God's ways and gave Him praise for His greatness. He then continued by asking God to remember MERCY when He has to bring wrath. Not long after, the Southern Kingdom DID fall to the Babylonians, and many were taken captive. However, God's purposes would still be fulfilled.

ZEPHANIAH
Old Testament "Minor Prophet" Book
— SHAKE THE PEOPLE OUT OF COMPLACENCY AND BACK TO GOD —

The Book of Zephaniah: The book of Zephaniah shows how this Prophet from the Southern Kingdom of Judah was one who thundered warnings in order to bring his people back to God from their pagan worship. Obviously his warnings were not heeded. Soon after these words of warning, Judah was conquered by Babylon and some were carried into captivity. In spite of his words of caution, it was too late to stop the destruction. He ends by trying to restore hope in his people after they were purified.

HAGGAI
Old Testament "Minor Prophet" Book
— CALL TO THE PEOPLE TO CHANGE PRIORITIES AND REBUILD THE TEMPLE —

The Book of Haggai: Haggai changed Jerusalem. He encouraged the 50,000 Jewish exiles who returned from captivity in Babylon to rebuild Jerusalem. The work had begun but stopped – and after 15 years only the Temple foundation was completed. For four months, Haggai challenged the priorities of the people because they were living in nice homes while the Temple was still in ruins. Because they decided to listen and heed his words, the Temple was completed four years later.

Haggai encouraged them by letting them know that even though this Temple was not as grand as Solomon's Temple had been before its destruction, God's presence would still be there and, God's people would have an incredible future.

ZECHARIAH
Old Testament "Minor Prophet" Book
— GOD BRINGS HOPE OF DELIVERANCE THROUGH THE FUTURE MESSIAH —

The Book of Zechariah: The book of Zechariah brings to us a Prophet who was one of the 50,000 people who had returned to Jerusalem from Babylonian exile. Zechariah's name means "The Lord Remembers!" God DID remember to bring His people back into their land of promise. He warns them that the KEY to God's blessing is OBEDIENCE.

Zechariah predicts more of the coming Messiah than any other Prophet except Isaiah. He also informs the Israelites that there was a greater plan ahead for them and that their KING was coming. We notice that Zechariah speaks of both Christ's first coming and then also His second coming when He returns to earth for His millennial reign. Zechariah wrote of Christ's first coming 500 years before its fulfillment.

MALACHI
Old Testament "Minor Prophet" Book
— CONFRONTS SIN AND URGES RESTORATION OF RELATIONSHIP WITH GOD —

The Book of Malachi: The book of Malachi tells that about 100 years had passed since the Jewish people had returned to their land from their Babylonian captivity. The Temple had now been rebuilt, but over time, the people did not take their worship seriously. The Priests and the people were cheating God by not giving Him the offerings that were due Him. Another conundrum was that they were now also beginning to marry outside the people of God – becoming unequally yoked. The Prophet Malachi warned that if they did not repent, then the Lord would have to judge and purify His people again.

What a shame to see that again the nation had forgotten God! Only through repentance and reformation would the people experience God's Blessing. Malachi reassures and also warns his people that this great and dreadful day of the Lord was coming. Unfortunately, almost 400 years would go by with NO WORD from God until the Angel Gabriel announced the birth of John the Baptist, who would prepare the way for Jesus, the Messiah.

Chapter Twenty-Two

— THE FOUR GOSPELS OF THE NEW TESTAMENT —

The New Testament tells a new and climactic part of the continuing story of how God lovingly pursued intimacy with all people. Due to God's great love, He gave His only son, Jesus Christ, to die on the Cross, in order to establish a new promise. This was to be our New Covenant, a covenant that allows each of us redemption and the ability to return to God.

There had been no word from God since the Prophet Malachi. The 400 years of SILENCE was broken with the announcement of the coming Messiah, whose name was to be Jesus. Jesus was the one delegated to pay the penalty for the betrayal that Adam fell into back in the Garden of Eden, the place where all authority had been handed over to satan.

Jesus, paying this debt, took that authority from satan and brought it back to God where it belonged, bringing us a New Covenant. In this way, He became the Redeemer and Savior for those who would choose to believe in Him. The four Gospels tell of Jesus' life and His deeds.

MATTHEW

— WRITES THIS GOSPEL TO THE JEWISH COMMUNITY —

<u>Matthew</u>: This Gospel was penned by Matthew. He was not only a tax collector, but also one of the eye witness disciples in the life of Jesus. Matthew focuses on the fulfillment of the Old Testament Prophecies confirming to the Jewish audience how the Old Testament KEY <u>promises</u> have been linked to the New Testament <u>fulfillment</u>. You see, the Jewish people had waited for a Messiah Who would rescue them from Roman activity and establish a kingdom like David's from long ago.

Here, Matthew is determined to make sure that they understand that the Messiah, Who has been prophesied from the beginning of time, and Whom they had been looking for, had indeed made His appearance. Matthew purposes to answer any questions about Jesus' claim to be the Messiah. He proves that Jesus was the predicted King, but explains why Jesus did not form the kind of kingdom that they had expected.

Matthew begins his Gospel by tracing Joseph's genealogy all the way back to Abraham. Joseph was of the "<u>Royal Line</u>" of David with the monarchy ending with Jeconiah, an evil and idolatrous king – therefore, Joseph, who <u>could</u> have been a <u>king</u>, was only a carpenter. Matthew shows that Jesus was truly a man from Israel, and thus His teaching also is one that is fully in the rightful custom of Israel's teaching of the law. Matthew is the only Gospel in which Jesus says He has not come to dissolve the law but to fulfill it, and that no part of the law will disappear.

In *Matthew 5:1,* Jesus went up to the mountain to give the Sermon on the Mount to His people. This was important to the Jewish people as God [Jesus] speaks from the mountain top. Moses went to the top of Mount Sinai to have God speak with him. He meant for the Jewish people to be able to equate Jesus with the God Who gave the Ten Commandments from the mountain.

MARK

— WROTE THIS GOSPEL TO THE NON-JEWISH COMMUNITY —

<u>Mark:</u> The Gospel of Mark was meant to be for the Roman audience and non-Jewish readers who needed to hear the facts surrounding Jesus' life, death, and resurrection. Mark delivers the good news about Jesus like a reporter. He basically outlines the life events and actions of Jesus. Details of interest to the Jewish leaders are not found in Mark's Gospel. There was no genealogy needed to prove Jesus' right to the throne and you will not find criticism of Israel's religious leaders. In contrast, Matthew's Gospel reasons with the Jewish minds to prove Jesus' authenticity.

John Mark, mostly referred to as "Mark," was not an Apostle, but spent much time with Peter. Mark was able to collect information from him, and then assemble it into what is known as the Gospel of Mark. It was thought to be Mark's parents' home where Jesus and the disciples ate the "Last Supper," also known as the "Passover Seder Meal."

Mark emphasizes the fact that Jesus came as the suffering Servant and not as a conquering King, but one willing to sacrifice His life for us (God's Plan "B"). One third of this Gospel speaks of His suffering and death.

LUKE

— A GREEK PHYSICIAN —
— AFFIRMS JESUS' DIVINITY —

<u>Luke:</u> The Gospel of Luke was written by a Greek physician named Luke, probably the only non-Jewish writer in the New Testament. He was not an eye witness, but he researched and recorded much of the surroundings of Jesus, beginning with the prophesied prediction of the coming birth of Jesus Christ to the death, resurrection, and ascension of the Messiah.

The largest amount of detail surrounding the birth of Jesus is in Luke's Gospel. Luke traces Mary's genealogy all the way back to the first man, Adam, which was considered the "<u>Blood Line.</u>" You will notice that women were not recognized in that genealogy, so instead of seeing Mary's name listed as the mother of Jesus, you will see Jesus, as the son of *"Joseph, the son of Eli,"* because he [Joseph] had married Mary.

The "<u>Royal Line of David</u>" and the "<u>Blood Line</u>" separates with Solomon and Nathan, David's two sons. Solomon carried the <u>Royal</u> Line, ending with Joseph, while Nathan carried the <u>Blood</u> Line, ending with Mary.

Luke accompanied Paul on his missionary journeys and thus, also authored the Book of "Acts," recollecting much of his first hand experiences. While Luke was with the Apostle Paul in Jerusalem, he virtually had access to each of the disciples, as well as Mary, the mother of Jesus. From that, he gleaned his information, beginning with the virgin birth, the events and teachings of Jesus, all the way to the Cross and the Ascension.

According to Luke, Jesus was the one who had lived a perfect life, which was needed in order to fulfill God's plan "B." He then became the perfect Sacrifice that could overthrow satan and redeem us from everlasting damnation, due to the high treason committed in the Garden of Eden. We now have access to live with God throughout eternity, thanks to Jesus!

Luke wrote this Gospel for the helpless, confused, and lost people of any era. At the heart of this Gospel, we see the comparison of Jesus as the pursuing Savior, where He is likened to someone searching for a lost coin, lost sheep, and a lost son.

JOHN

—DISCLOSES JESUS' IDENTITY THROUGHOUT THIS GOSPEL —

<u>John:</u> The Gospel of John was meant for those who are "Born Again Christians," repeatedly speaking of the giving of the Holy Spirit by God, and the need for believers to have a Spiritual personal relationship! John writes to all the churches, as Gnosticism was trying to infiltrate the churches. Having been considered the best friend of Jesus, John's goal was to prove that Jesus IS GOD, and wanted to make sure that His Word is clear!

John had originally been a follower of John the Baptist. It is believed that John was present when the Dove came down as Jesus was baptized, and he would have heard the voice of God proclaiming, *"This is My Beloved Son, in whom I am well pleased!" Matthew 3:17.* Immediately after, John and Andrew became disciples of Jesus, followed by Peter and John's brother, James. John focuses on the spiritual truths that we are to learn from the accounts of Jesus' teachings and death on the Cross.

John's powerful argument is that the Creator became a part of His creation. To say that God came to earth, taking on flesh and bone, needed explanation. This Gospel brings out that Jesus was indeed "Deity" in the flesh. John shows this by listing the miraculous signs that Jesus performed, confirming the identity of Jesus, and present Him as the ONLY source to eternal life.

God's love was the motive for limiting Himself to time and space. A point John makes is that Jesus, as a man, even aged, and was susceptible to sickness and death like any of us. However, His purpose was also to let us know that He was God in the flesh.

Every chapter depicts the revelation of God. Some miraculous signs are:

- Turning water into wine
- Healing groups of people
- Feeding the 5000 with just a few loaves and two fish
- Feeding the 4000
- Walking on water
- Restoring sight to the blind
- Raising Lazarus from the dead
- Giving disciples an enormous catch of fish
- His own resurrection.

John emphasizes the "Way of Salvation!" He lists eye witnesses who could vouch that they saw Jesus after His resurrection. All these signs were to confirm Jesus' own words:

- *John 6:35, "I am the Bread of Life!"*
- *John 8:12, "I am the Light of the World!"*
- *John 11:25 "I am the Resurrection and the Life!"*

Chapter Twenty-Three

— HISTORY THROUGH THE
ACTS OF THE APOSTLES —

A cts: Also known as "The Acts of the Apostles," this book covers the first thirty years of church history and tells what happened to Jesus' disciples after Jesus returned to Heaven. We are shown how the Christians triumphed in spite of the opposition as well as persecutions they had to endure. Despite the consequences of the enemy's constant tactics towards Christendom, God sent His Holy Spirit to empower the believers, who then began meeting together on a regular basis.

This was the beginning of what is now known as "The Church." As they came together, they began to receive insight as to how to overcome all obstacles by receiving the Baptism of the Holy Spirit and with tenacity spread God's Word throughout the Roman Empire. They experienced healings as they laid hands on the sick throughout the region or wherever God would send them.

God's final promise to His disciples was that they would receive power to be His witnesses throughout the land and to the ends of the earth. Therefore, the course of history did change as the Book of Acts shows God's standards for the church.

— WHO WAS THE APOSTLE PAUL? —

The Apostle Paul, originally known as Saul of Tarsus, was a Jewish zealot, who had been taught in the finest rabbinical school by a Pharisee named Gamaliel. Saul truly believed that the Christians were a detriment to God and needed to be destroyed. Though his motive was genuine, the enemy used Saul, so sincere and devout, to try to get rid of believers. Again, God intervened. God met him one day as Saul was headed for Damascus to annihilate more of those he considered his enemy. Saul became blinded and then God revealed Himself to him. As a result, Saul was converted to Christendom and his name was changed to Paul. *(Acts 22)*

Chapter Twenty-Four

ROMANS
A New Testament Epistle

— MANKIND'S NATURE COMES FROM ADAM'S REBELLION AGAINST GOD —

Romans: This epistle of Paul's is the longest and most influential letter written to the newly formed church in Rome, which was founded by other believers. Paul shares the meaning of a transformed life in Christ, how that life results in righteousness, and receiving revelation to God's mysteries.

Paul focuses on how satan does whatever he can in order to bring out the natural tendency to sin, this same sin that lives within every person's heart since the fall of Adam. But, that God plans for redemption to come full-circle. All that is necessary is for mankind to make the CHOICE to receive Jesus as their Lord and Savior.

I and II CORINTHIANS

— LOVE, LIFE STYLE AND WORD OF RECONCILIATION —

I and II Corinthians: Corinth, an Ancient city in Greece, was morally corrupt, and was known as the sensual city. Because the church was made up of many ex-pagan Gentiles, it was running rampant with sin. Therefore, Paul had to address the kinds of problems that any church experiences when its members are what one would call "worldly."

It was nothing for prostitutes to try to sell themselves even after they became a part of the church, because of their culture, and therefore Paul had to correct the sensual problems as well as counsel and instruct the people of Corinth.

In his second letter to Corinth, we see where some were challenging Paul's authority and questioning his honesty to the church in Corinth. Paul has to expose the false apostles who continue to speak against him and who were trying to undermine his integrity, as well as distort his message of the Gospel.

He also has to reprimand those in the church who were allowing the influence of Paul's foes to sway them. Paul diligently teaches them the truth and ends by encouraging them to be committed to God's Word.

GALATIANS

— SALVATION APART FROM WORKS —

Galatians: Paul speaks to the Galatians about what is required for mankind to be redeemed. Some of the Jewish teachers were unsettling the new believers by insisting that it was important for them to be circumcised and still remain under the Mosaic Law. He then addresses the question of how non-Jewish Gentile believers could relate to the Jewish Laws. Most of the early followers of Jesus were Jewish; having been taught the Torah, but now had claimed Jesus as their Messiah. As a result, they struggled with this dual identity.

Their Jewish heritage, as well as their understanding that Jesus was indeed the Messiah, brought them even closer to their Mosaic Law. Though they desired to follow the Mosaic Law more closely, they found that their new faith in Christ also brought them liberty. This was a result of the love that Jesus had taught.

They also were perplexed as to how non-Jewish Gentiles could possibly become a part of Heaven. Paul explains that WORKS will not bring anyone to salvation, and that any religion depending on human effort definitely is NOT salvation, as that system would deny the finished work of Christ's death and resurrection. Only the Holy Spirit can make us better than we are. Paul explains that God's grace in Christ is the New Covenant that can bring us to salvation.

Chapter Twenty-Five

— LETTERS KNOWN AS THE "PRISON" EPISTLES —
Written by Paul from Prison

EPHESIANS
— WORD OF TRUTH —

Ephesians: Located in the city of Ephesus, on the coast of what is now Turkey, this church was considered one of the most prominent ones to which Paul wrote. In this city, the Apostle John is believed to have lived, taking care of Mary, the mother of Jesus, until her death.

In this letter to the people of Ephesus, Paul defines the meaning of "Predestination!" So often – even in today's society, we hear people saying that if we are all "predestined" to go to Heaven or hell, then what difference does it make how we live? However, it is important to note that the PLAN is what is predestined and foreknown, NOT the individual conformity to the plan. *Romans 8:29-30 says, "For whom He foreknew, He also predestined to become conformed to the image of His Son, that He might be the first-born among many brethren, and whom He predestined, these He also called, and whom He called, these He also justified; and whom He justified, these He also glorified."*

This means God has <u>called all of mankind,</u> giving each one of us the FREE WILL to choose to accept or reject His call. Those who accept, "<u>He has foreknown and predestined</u>" will be made righteous. Those who reject, "<u>He has foreknown and predestined</u>" will be consigned to eternal hell. In *Ephesians 1:5* he tells us that *"He predestined us to adoption as sons through Jesus Christ to Himself, according to the kind intention of His will...."*

This is what God thought of when He went to Plan "B" in Genesis. From the very beginning it was always His desire to have us choose to accept His call.

PHILIPPIANS

— WORD OF LIFE —

<u>Philippians</u>: Paul expresses thanks to the people of Philippi for their support of him and stresses that joy can be found in any situation. You have to remember that he is imprisoned in Rome at the time he is writing this. Paul basically points out that joy is that quiet assurance and confidence of God's love that we can all have in our lives, no matter what the circumstances are around us.

Paul warns the people of Philippi of self-seeking attitudes. Through it all, he always lifted up Jesus' model of having a humble attitude, and reminds the believers that Jesus will always set aside whatever is necessary for them. Paul ends by saying that he considers everything a loss compared to the surpassing greatness of knowing Christ Jesus, his Lord. Should we not do the same?

I would like to interject here that the Epistles have really come alive to my husband and me, due to our being privileged to having our home base with dear friends in Athens for two weeks while visiting Greece and the Grecian Islands. Having seen the archeological ruins of Ephesus, Philippi, and Corinth, visiting friends in Cenchrea, which is near Corinth where Paul sailed out with Aquila and Priscilla (*Acts 18:18*), then seeing Thessalonica, as well as Mars Hill and the Acropolis in Athens (*Acts 17:16*), and hearing natives speaking of their Biblical history, has made these letters from Paul very real and dear to us.

COLOSSIANS

— EXPOSED HELLENISTIC HERESIES —

Colossians: This letter, also written by Paul, is similar to the one he wrote to Ephesus while he was imprisoned in Rome. Colossae is located in what is currently Turkey. Again, satan brings about false teachers who would try to confuse the new believers with teachings that were contradictory to Biblical truths. This is a continual pattern in satan's scheme to destroy God's Word and works, trying to diminish Jesus' deity.

Paul concludes by stressing the true nature of a new life in Christ, as well as its demands on the believer, and strongly affirms Christ's full deity. This is quite the contrast to the accusations made by modern day non-believers who claim that the Bible is merely a "crutch" for "weaklings!"

THESSALONIANS

— ENCOURAGEMENT AND DEDICATION —

I and II Thessalonians: Thessalonica is a city located in northern Greece, and it was the second place where Paul preached the Gospel. Some of the Jewish people who lived there were not happy with Paul and came to oppose him, ultimately persecuting him to the point where Paul had no choice but to leave quite abruptly. His young converts, Timothy being one of them, received only minimal instructions and yet, when persecution came – their faith and zeal blessed Paul. He wrote to commend them for their perseverance in the midst of their persecutions. Most of these new believers had come from pagan backgrounds, so he encouraged and instructed them in Godly living.

Paul gives a glimpse of what will transpire when the last trumpet sounds and the dead in Christ shall rise, followed by the Rapture of the church. *I Thessalonians 4:13-18, "But we do not want you to be uninformed, brethren, about those who are asleep, so that you will not grieve as do the rest who have no hope. For if we believe that Jesus died and rose again, even so God will bring with Him those who have fallen asleep in Jesus."*

"For this we say to you by the word of the Lord, that we, who are alive and remain until the coming of the Lord, will not precede those who have fallen asleep. For the Lord Himself will descend from Heaven with a shout, with the voice of the archangel and with the trumpet of God, and the dead in Christ will rise first."

"Then we who are alive and remain will be caught up together [Raptured] with them in the clouds to meet the Lord in the air, and so we shall always be with the Lord. Therefore comfort one another with these words."

Another subject that had perplexed the new believers was the assurance of the future of believers who die before Christ returns. Each chapter touches on the fact that Christ will return, giving hope to all believers who are burdened by grief and sorrow.

The second letter to the Thessalonians addresses the confusion which arose about the End-Time happenings related to *"the day of the Lord" (2:2)*. Some felt that God's judgment had already begun and were confused about the time of Christ's return. Interestingly, there were those who had even stopped working because of that confusion. So, Paul thought it imperative that he respond quickly.

2 Thessalonians 2:1-4 says, "Now we request you, brethren, with regard to the coming of our Lord Jesus Christ and our gathering together to Him, that you not be quickly shaken from your composure or be disturbed either by a spirit or a message or a letter as if from us, to the effect that the day of the Lord has come."

"Let no one in any way deceive you, for it will not come unless the apostasy comes first, and the man of lawlessness is revealed, the son of destruction, who opposes and exalts himself above every so-called god or object of worship, so that he takes his seat in the temple of God, displaying himself as being God."

Paul then continues to encourage them as to how to live UNTIL the day of Christ's return. *2 Thessalonians 3:3-6 states, "The Lord is faithful, and He will strengthen and protect you from the evil one. We have confidence in the Lord concerning you that you are doing and will continue to do what we command. May the Lord direct your hearts into the love of God and into the steadfastness of Christ! Now we command you, brethren, in the name of our Lord Jesus Christ that you keep away from every brother who leads an unruly life and not according to the tradition which you received from us."*

Chapter Twenty-Six

— LETTERS KNOWN AS THE "PASTORAL" EPISTLES —
Concerning Pastoral Care to Churches and Qualifications for Ministers

I and II TIMOTHY

— SHOWS HOW ALL SCRIPTURE IS INSPIRED BY GOD —

I and II Timothy: Written by Paul, this letter was considered a "Leadership Manual" to Timothy, who was the first 2nd Generation believer noted in the New Testament. As a young minister of the Gospel, Timothy experienced considerable persecutions in the various churches. Paul urges Timothy to preserve the integrity of the Gospel and its holy standards from getting corrupted by these false teachers.

Having been imprisoned again in Rome under Nero, Paul writes this last but most intimate letter to his son in the Lord. Imagine, Paul, sitting in a cold cell, yet he takes the time to write and encourage Timothy in the faith.

Because of the problems Timothy had with the church in Ephesus, Paul instructs him in those issues and troubles. You see, satan was not giving up....and we know he never will. His intent is to do all he can to deceive mankind. *Whatever he has tried that has worked before, rest assured, he will continue to use over and over again.* He only gives up when it no longer works. To this day, deception and confusion is seen in the churches, and it is up to us to defend the church, the Gospel, and the Deity of Christ.

TITUS

— SPEAKS OF A PASTOR'S ROLE IN THE CHURCH STRUCTURE —

Titus: Titus was a Greek convert as a result of Paul's ministry. Paul and Titus had visited the Island of Crete, the fourth largest Island in the Mediterranean Sea, and introduced them to the Gospel of Jesus Christ.

Later on, Paul sent Titus back to the Island of Crete to finish the work that he [Paul] was unable to complete before his imprisonment. This work included the organizational task of appointing elders to the church, helping them to grow in faith and knowledge of God's Word, and finally, to put a stop to the false teachers.

PHILEMON

— RELATIONSHIP OF MASTER VERSUS SLAVE —

Philemon: Paul wrote a short letter to this believer from Colossae, in Asia Minor. This man, Philemon, had been a slave owner. It appears that Onesimus, one of his slaves, stole from him and then became a runaway slave who in that culture, was destined to be punished by death.

Onesimus had gone to see Paul in Rome and Paul was able to lead him to Christ. Now, Paul is interceding on his behalf and asks Philemon not only to take him back, but to treat him as a fellow believer and not as a slave. He proceeds to ask Philemon to love this man as he would have loved his friend, Paul. This is a beautiful story of forgiveness followed by total restoration.

A nother significant lesson here is that the name Onesimus means "useful," but he was actually <u>useless</u> while serving as a slave. After Paul led him to the Lord, he became "useful" to both Paul and Philemon.

Chapter Twenty-Seven

HEBREWS

— THE "MASTERFUL" DOCUMENT, GOD'S WORD IS ALIVE AND POWERFUL —

<u>H</u>ebrews: This author wrote to the Jewish people who struggled with their new faith. Some have claimed that this is the writing of Paul, however, no one really knows for sure. Judaism expressed true devotion to the God of Abraham, Isaac, and Jacob. The Mosaic Law, the Ten Commandments, the rituals, as well as the Prophets of Old, all illustrate God's promises, showing the Israelites the way to forgiveness and salvation. Missing, however, was an understanding that when Jesus, the Messiah, came to redeem mankind, He also came to FULFILL the "Law and the Prophets."

He came to break down all strongholds, open the floodgates to God, provide eternal redemption, and prepare a life with God in His heavenly home. This is destined to be forever and ever to all who believe in Him and receive Him as their personal Savior and Lord.

Even though the Israelites had been looking earnestly for the Messiah for centuries, Jesus was very difficult for them to accept. It is understandable for them to have had difficulty comprehending their new faith. We have all experienced the task of having to UNDO years of teaching in our minds and then try to change our thinking to a new concept we are supposed to now learn. This is called TRADITION!

Hebrews 6:13-18 gives us a glimpse of what God intended to do. *"For when God made the promise to Abraham, since He could swear by no one greater, He swore by Himself, saying, 'I WILL SURELY BLESS YOU AND I WILL SURELY MULTIPLY YOU.' And so, having patiently waited, Abraham obtained the promise. For men swear by one greater than themselves, and with them an oath given as confirmation is an end of every dispute. In the same way God, desiring even more to show to the heirs of the promise the unchangeableness of His purpose, interposed with an oath, so that by two unchangeable things in which it is impossible for God to lie, we who have taken refuge would have strong encouragement to take hold of the hope set before us."*

The nature of the Glory of God [Blessing], was to produce the Garden of Eden and expand it. There was enough power in that Blessing to multiply and be fruitful. The original intent was the whole earth was to become the "Garden of Eden." Had Adam not sinned and KEPT the Blessing God *had sworn by Himself to him*, the rest of the Bible would never have been necessary, and all offspring would have walked as they did at the very beginning....with God.

What did the writer of Hebrews mean when he said that God "swore by Himself?" It merely meant that it was a "Blood Oath" that has with it a death sentence in it when broken. The KJV says it this way, *"Wherein God, willing more abundantly to shew unto the heirs of promise the immutability of his counsel, confirmed it by an oath."(17)*

Immutability is defined to mean "the divine attribute of unchangeableness." God said in *Exodus 3:14, "I AM that I AM,"* signifying His eternal sameness and His sovereignty.

He cannot change His moral character, His love, His omni-science, omnipresence, omnipotence, etc. God is *"From everlasting to everlasting," (Psalm 90:2)*. In other words, He will not change His mind. What He says, He means. What He means, He says. This Blessing to Adam was a "Blood Sworn Oath." Jesus became that "Blood Sworn Oath" Who took on flesh and dwelt among us.

The Book of Hebrews tries to explain the superiority and completion of God's revelation and redemption in Jesus Christ. The provisions, under the Old Covenant, have been fulfilled and made obsolete by Jesus' coming. The New Covenant was established through the atoning death of Jesus. The writer appeals to the believer to hold on to their confession of Christ until the end. He also encourages each believer to do all they can to mature spiritually, abiding in God's Word, and to never abandon the faith. Are we living as though Jesus is better than any other way of life? If not, then why?

Chapter Twenty-Eight

JAMES

— KNOWN AS THE "GENERAL LETTER" —
Originally addressed to a wider audience,
not just to a local church.

<u>J</u>ames: Many believe that this book was written by James,
the half-brother of Jesus. At first, James was like any
other brother who did not really believe in Jesus, and even
challenged him. Later he became a believer and grew to be
faithful in the church, as we see in this written letter.

The salutation of this letter, which addresses "the twelve
tribes, who are scattered among the nations," shows that it
was written to Jewish Christians living outside Palestine.
Perhaps the writer tried to exhort those who were among
the first believers in Jerusalem, but then scattered at the time
that Stephen was martyred. *Acts 7:54-8:3, "...Now when
they heard this, they were cut to the quick, and they began
gnashing their teeth at Stephen. But being full of the Holy
Spirit, he gazed intently into Heaven and saw the glory of
God, and Jesus standing at the right hand of God; and he
said, "Behold, I see the Heavens opened up and the Son of*

Man standing at the right hand of God." But they cried out with a loud voice, and covered their ears and rushed at him with one impulse."

"When they had driven him out of the city, they began stoning him; and the witnesses laid aside their robes at the feet of a young man named Saul. They went on stoning Stephen as he called on the Lord and said, "Lord Jesus, receive my spirit!" Then falling on his knees, he cried out with a loud voice, "Lord, do not hold this sin against them!" Having said this, he fell asleep. Saul was in hearty agreement with putting him to death, and on that day a great persecution began against the church in Jerusalem, and they were all scattered throughout the regions of Judea and Samaria, except the apostles. Some devout men buried Stephen, and made loud lamentation over him. But Saul began ravaging the church, entering house after house, and dragging off men and women, he would put them in prison."

James was trying to encourage the believers to do all they could to endure any trials that might come their way and benefit from them. He calls them to resist temptations and become doers of the Word.

In these chapters he also teaches about how an unruly tongue can hurt us; why we need worldly wisdom; understanding sinful behavior; and the danger of self-centered wealth. He then summarizes his book with the emphasis on patience and being diligent in prayer. These are vital lessons for us all to learn.

The most ineffective Christians are those who are only hearers and never DO anything. Satan just loves Christians who can quote hundreds of Scriptures, keep up with the best of scholars, and yet, live a life under his jurisdiction. As long as satan can keep them confused, they are no threat to him at all. Sadder yet, they are of no assistance whatsoever to the Kingdom of God.

<u>Is it possible for a Christian to become an enemy of</u>
<u>God?</u>
Excerpts from Rick Renner's "Sparkling Gems from the
Greek" June 23rd Devotional

> Based on *James 4:4-6, "You adulteresses, do you*
> *not know that friendship with the world is hostility*
> *(enmity) toward God? Therefore whoever wishes to*
> *be a friend of the world makes himself an enemy of*
> *God. Or do you think that the Scripture speaks to no*
> *purpose: He jealously desires the Spirit which He has*
> *made to dwell in us? But He gives a greater grace.*
> *Therefore it says, "GOD IS OPPOSED TO THE*
> *PROUD, BUT GIVES GRACE TO THE HUMBLE."*

"How does God view a believer who once walked
with Him and knew the power of the Holy Spirit but
has now become so entangled in the world that he
hardly ever picks up his Bible to read it, rarely prays,
and only comes to church if it "fits" into his sched-
uled of things to do?

The word "enemy" in the Greek [*echthros*]
denotes hostility, antagonism, and even animosity for
each other. Therefore in *verse 4*, it is unquestionable,
as it is a picture of a hostile force. James uses this
word to express the feelings and emotions that God
possesses toward a believer who transfers his devotion and passion from Him to the world. By using
this word, James tells us that if a believer chooses to
make his relationship with the world a greater priority
than his relationship with God, he is making a choice
that will put him in direct opposition to God. In fact,
the word *echthros* lets us know that God takes this
decision so personally that He views it as an act of
war! To God, *this is the ultimate violation*!

To truly serve God, you must spend time with Him so you can know His voice and develop a pattern of obedience in your daily walk. It will demand your fullest attention. The work of God must be "serviced" with prayer, obedience, repentance, and worship.

If a person chooses to serve mammon [worldliness] instead of the Lord (*Matthew 6:24*), he will have to turn his attention and devotion to the world. As a worldly person, he will be required to learn the ways of the world and to adapt to the thinking of the world. Serving the world and worldliness requires 100 percent of a person's attention.

Just as serving God requires your time, attention, energy, and money, the world will demand the same from you. This is why Jesus said it is not possible to serve both God and mammon. You see, there is just not enough of you to serve both of these masters simultaneously, so you must choose whom you are going to serve.

If you are consumed with God, these other things will take a lower place on your list of priorities. But if you are consumed with the world, material things will dominate the landscape of your mind.

James 4:6 tells us that God takes a stand against a believer who turns his devotions to the world and becomes worldly. In fact, it says God "resists" such believers. The word "resist" in Greek is a military term that means to *militarily order one's self against someone else*. This is no accidental, fly-by-night plan of resistance, but a well-planned, prepared resistance.

This emphatically declares that God takes it so personally when a believer turns his devotion from Him to the world that He sets Himself in opposition to that believer. Like a military commander, God reviews the situation: then He decides how to resist and frustrate the things this believer is trying to achieve and thus bring him to a place of surrender.

If this believer does not quickly surrender, repent, and come back to where he ought to be, God will continue to take a stand against his activities. The Christian can rebuke the devil all day long, but it will be to no avail, for his problem is not the devil – his problem is God.

As terrible as this resistance sounds it is a manifestation of God's grace! By blocking our way and resisting our choices, the precious Holy Spirit endeavors to get our attention and to bring us to a sweet place of brokenness, where sin is confessed and fellowship with God is restored.

You see, God is so passionate about your relationship with Him that He is unwilling to share you with the world. That does not mean you cannot have a job or be successful. In most cases, you must have a job, and God wants you to be successful. But if you switch your allegiance from God to the world around you, God views that as the ultimate violation in His sight. It is the very act that causes Him to decide to rise up and to do something to bring you back to where you ought to be!"

This is a perfect description of how satan tries to keep Christians ineffective. There are so many who call themselves Christians in this day and age, and yet the non-Christians would never know, as they see those who call themselves Christians living no differently than they are. Be aware of the enemy's course of action, because he will do what he must. If the enemy cannot succeed in keeping a person out of Heaven, he will surely do all he can to keep that person in bondage, whether it be poverty, sickness, depression, or addiction.

Chapter Twenty-Nine

— PETER'S LETTERS TO THE SUFFERING CHURCH —
In Asia Minor

I Peter: Peter knew what it meant to deny Jesus. He also had a great understanding of what it meant to endure beatings, not to mention seeing his friends die and the church scattered. Oh! But Peter KNEW Christ, and there was nothing that could shatter his confidence in his risen Lord. He basically warns of persecutions that come from those <u>outside</u> the church.

Peter reminds believers that we have a glorious calling and Heavenly inheritance in Jesus. He emphasizes that this great salvation was foreseen by the Prophets of the Old Testament and that it is imperative that Christians live holy lives. Believers need the pure milk of the Word to grow from infancy, but then they are to mature with the meat of the Word.

Peter stresses the truth that believers are aliens and strangers on earth, but encourages them to keep their focus, like a flint, onto their Heavenly home. He concludes this first letter by stating that those who suffer with Christ will become partners with the ONE who suffered, namely Christ.

II Peter: This letter was written close to the time when Peter would be martyred in Rome by dying upside down on a cross. He warns of false teachers <u>within</u> the church, who can be subtly deceitful, having impure selfish motives. The enemy is out there to deceive and ultimately destroy even those who purpose to be sold out to Christendom. Therefore, Peter urges the believers to pursue godliness and to be on their guard, ready to expose those who have come into their midst whose objective is to undermine God's Word.

With only five more books of the Bible remaining, my prayer is that you can now see a pattern (cycle) showing how God not only warns us of the quest of the enemy, but also tells us of the assurance of what God plans on doing to accomplish His plan "B." The thought of having all this knowledge and information available and still have the reader walk away from it in disbelief is totally bewildering to me. Oh, if this book could open the eyes of those who were duped into thinking that only the New Testament is of importance and the Old Testament is no longer necessary to read.

If someone has never taken the time to read the Bible in a topical fashion and has depended upon others interpretation of the conglomerates accumulated throughout their adult years, then they could be swayed into believing the Bible is a myth! This indeed would keep that person from understanding the full plan of God and His reasons for doing what He must.

Chapter Thirty

I, II, AND III JOHN

— REASSURES CHRISTIANS IN THEIR FAITH, COUNTERS FALSE TEACHINGS —

I <u>John</u>: John, the disciple of Christ, who spent time on the Isle of Patmos, is the author of this letter, as well as the Gospel of John and the Book of Revelation. In this letter, his goal is to remove any doubts as to who Jesus was and is. You see, he was the one who walked and talked with Jesus and was considered the most beloved disciple. John saw Jesus die, ran to His grave with Peter the morning that He had arisen, spent time with Him after His resurrection, and finally saw Christ's ascension into Heaven. He is also the one whom Jesus spoke to from the Cross when He said, *"Behold your Mother"* (*John 19:26-27*). This is the same John who took care of Jesus' mother in Ephesus during her old age.

Also in this letter – John assures the 'Children of God' of their salvation. *I John 5:10-12. "The one who believes in the Son of God has the testimony in himself; the one who does not believe God has made Him a liar, because he has not believed in the testimony that God has given concerning His Son. And the testimony is this that God has given us eternal life, and this life is in His Son. He who has the Son has the life; he who does not have the Son of God does not have the life."*

Again, we see the warning of false teachers who are at work (John calls them antichrists), trying to discredit Christ's deity. Confusion will always lead one astray, and in this case we see immorality. John corrects false teachings, and with great love for these people assures them of the truth about Jesus Christ.

II John: John was in Ephesus when he wrote this letter. We see in these writings how necessary the fundamentals are for living a Christ-like life. Again, he is doing his best to protect the young churches from the onslaught of the false teachers permeating the area. You see, false teachings will ultimately harm its victims for eternity. John has the tenacity to do what he can to protect the new churches.

II John 1:6-9, "And this is love that we walk according to His commandments... that you should walk in it. For many deceivers have gone out into the world, those who do not acknowledge Jesus Christ as coming in the flesh. This is the deceiver and the antichrist. Watch yourselves that you do not lose what we have accomplished, but that you may receive a full reward. Anyone who goes too far and does not abide in the teaching of Christ, does not have God; the one who abides in the teaching, he has both the Father and the Son." His focus is to live in love, obedience, and truth.

III John: Gaius was a man who showed hospitality to traveling missionaries and teachers. This letter was written to him, not only praising him for his generosity, but also warning Gaius of a man who was unwilling to listen to spiritual leadership. *III John 9-11 says, "I wrote something to the church; but Diotrephes, who loves to be first among them, does not accept what we say. For this reason, if I come, I will call attention to his deeds which he does, unjustly accusing us with wicked words; and not satisfied with this, he himself does not receive the brethren, either, and he forbids those who desire to do so and puts them out of the church. Beloved, do not imitate what is evil, but what is good. The one who does good is of God; the one who does evil has not seen God."*

Why are we surprised to hear that satan's quest has not, nor will it end? He is determined, but we must never forget that from the very onset, God declared that he <u>will</u> be defeated. The enemy can only bring us down to his level if we allow him to.

Chapter Thirty-One

JUDE

— KEEP STRONG IN THE FAITH – OPPOSE HERESY —

Jude: Jude was another half brother of Jesus and the brother of James. This is a very brief but poignant letter of only 25 verses. Jude reiterates how God brought the Children of Israel out of Egypt (*Exodus 3*), and how He had to destroy those who did not believe (*Numbers 32*). He speaks of Cain, who murdered his brother (*Genesis 4:1-6*), of Balaam's error (*Number 22-24*), and Korah's rebellion (*Numbers 16*). Then he reminds us of the angels who were thrown out of Heaven (*Isaiah 14*), and their upcoming doom at the Great White Throne Judgment. Jude mentions how Sodom and Gomorrah (*Genesis 19*), with their sexual immorality, will be exhibited as an example of those who will undergo the punishment of the "Lake of Fire" for eternity. Later, Jude also warns the churches of those false teachers that were running rampant in their community and urges the believers to fight for the faith that had been carefully handed down to them.

In studying the book of Jude, and knowing that the enemy is still deceiving God's people, we too, must understand the need to stand firm in our faith based on what has been carefully handed down to us in the Word of God. Jude ends with a blessing to all who will joyfully cling to God, the Father, through our Lord Jesus Christ.

Chapter Thirty-Two

THE "APOCALYPTIC" BOOK OF REVELATION

— REVEALS THE FULL IDENTITY OF CHRIST — — GIVES WARNING AND HOPE TO BELIEVERS —

<u>The Book of Revelation</u>: We discover that John, the writer, shares his vision which he had received at the Isle of Patmos with the seven churches in the province of Asia. Five of those churches had serious internal problems with their disloyalty to Christ. He was deeply concerned about the heresy – probably Gnosticism – that overwhelmed the churches.

The Gnostics were a group of Christians who claimed to have a special revelation from God that allowed them to also dabble in the Roman civil religion. They watered down the uniqueness of Christ and since they considered all matter to be evil, their behavior was colored by moral compromise. The Christians within these churches were also in severe danger because of the civil demand of emperor worship, beginning with Caesar Augustus (27-14 BC), which supposedly brought peace to the ancient world. Out of gratitude, the people began to deify the emperors who personified Roman peace. Basically, the Roman Empire was at war with the Christian church.

Throughout the study of this last book, we see the person of Jesus Christ, the Lamb, always central in action in the message. This essential truth gave inspiration and hope to the first-century Christians of the Roman world. This same truth fills the 21st century Christians with quiet confidence that Jesus Christ is with us now in our complex world. We can be certain that He will be with us and we with Him in that future place which is called the New Heaven and the New Earth.

John gives us a precise description in the Book of Revelation of what we are privileged to look for. To someone who has no personal relationship with Jesus Christ, their Promised Messiah, the information most likely is frightening and questionable. To the believer, the comparison of the Seven Feasts of God, some of the Old Testament Prophets such as *Isaiah, Daniel* and *Joel,* combined with *I Thessalonians 4*, brings an incredible peace.

Since the first four of the Seven Feasts of God (Passover, Unleavened Bread, First Fruits, and Pentecost) have already been fulfilled, we can be assured it is imminent that the three remaining <u>un</u>fulfilled Feasts will indeed <u>be</u> fulfilled as well.

<u>Feast of Trumpets</u>: The fifth Feast of God is called "Feast of Trumpets," also known as Rosh Hashanah and/or The Jewish New Year. During this time, we can expect to see the fulfillment of *I Thessalonians 4:13-18*, which says, *"But we do not want you to be uninformed, brethren, about those who are asleep, so that you will not grieve as do the rest who have no hope. For if we believe that Jesus died and rose again, even so God will bring with Him those who have fallen asleep in Jesus. For this we say to you by the word of*

the Lord, that we, who are alive and remain until the coming of the Lord, will not precede those who have fallen asleep."

"For the Lord Himself will descend from Heaven with a shout, with the voice of the archangel and with the trumpet of God, and the dead in Christ will rise first. Then we who are alive and remain will be caught up together with them in the clouds to meet the Lord in the air, and so we shall always be with the Lord. Therefore comfort one another with these words."

From this, we see that when the Trumpet sounds, the Lord descends from Heaven with a shout, at which point the "dead in Christ" will have their graves opened in order to rise first. Immediately following will be those "alive in Christ" that will be "caught up in the air." These believers will disappear as quickly as it takes to "blink an eye." This is known to be the "Rapture" which, in Greek means "to catch away."

After chapter four, the Book of Revelation no longer speaks of The Church. This tells us that the believers have all been translated [Raptured] out of the earth just prior to the signing of the peace treaty with the antichrist. (Authors who have books out on this subject are John Hagee, Grant Jeffrey, Tim LaHaye, Hal Lindsay, Perry Stone, and Jack Van Impe, to name a few. These are all recommended reading!)

— FIRST QUARTER —
Within the Seven Year Tribulation Period

The Day of Atonement: The sixth Feast of God, also known as the final "Day of Reckoning," marks the beginning of the tribulation period which will last for a period of seven years. During the first quarter, the antichrist comes on the scene to sign his "peace treaty."

Revelation 4 begins with the scene in Heaven, introducing us to the <u>Four Living Creatures</u>, the <u>Twenty-four
elders</u>, and the <u>Three Heavens:</u>

- *Atmospheric*, where the prince of power [satan] is
- *Stellar Heaven*, which is considered outer space
- *Heaven of God*, God's Throne Room

Revelation 5 speaks of the <u>Seven Sealed Scroll,</u> which
was in the hand of someone (God) who sat on the throne
looking for the One (Jesus) Who was worthy to break the
seal and open it. The Angel proclaimed that the Lamb who is
from the tribe of Judah, the Root of David, overcame, so as
to be worthy to open the book and the seven seals.

In *Revelation, chapter 4*, we see the Four Living Creatures
bowing before the throne and always worshipping the Lord:
(*Ezekiel, chapter 1*)

- The first living creature was like a Lion – denoting
  the Supreme Being among the Beasts, and considered the <u>noblest</u> of them all (some declare it also
  speaks of the Gospel of Mark)
- The second living creature like a Calf/Ox – epit-
  omizing the <u>strongest</u> among the laboring cattle
  (some state it also speaks of the Gospel of Luke)
- The third living creature had a face as a Man/Angel
  – signifying the <u>wisest</u> in all creation (some affirm
  it to speak of the Gospel of Matthew)
- The fourth living creature was like a flying Eagle
  – which stands for the <u>swiftest</u> of all birds (some
  proclaim it to speak of the Gospel of John)

In other words, the beasts represent a picture of all the
greatness, strength, and beauty of <u>nature</u>. Here, we see nature
praising God. Then, in the verses which follow, it speaks of

the <u>twenty-four elders</u> who are praising God. When we put the two pictures together we get the complete picture of both nature and man engaged in continual praise and adoration of God. The never-ending activity of nature under the hand of God is a continuous tribute of praise. Hallelujah!

In *Revelation, chapter 4,* we see the 24 elders bowing down and worshipping Him. There are various views as to who these 24 elders are. Some believe they are spirit beings whom God created to be His wise counselors. Others believe them to represent the 12 tribes of Judah and the 12 Apostles. Then there are those who are of the opinion that they are saved mortals from the tribulation, who appear to have an advisory role. However, they are unquestionably worshipers, even casting their crowns before the throne, saying, *"Worthy are Thou, our Lord and our God, to receive honor and glory and power, for Thou didst create all things..." Revelation 4:10-11*

Revelation 6 introduces us to the antichrist – via the <u>Four Horsemen of the Apocalypse</u>.

- The white horse represents the antichrist
- The red horse speaks of war
- The black horse represents famine
- The pale horse – death

The families who will be left behind when their loved ones disappear will by now take a deep look into this entire scenario. Many of them will determine that those family members whom they thought were trying to push religion down their throats must have had a relationship with this Jesus they spoke so freely about. During this time, many will make the decision to also serve Jesus and make Him the Lord of their lives. Also, during this time, many Jewish people will begin to understand that Jesus is indeed that Promised

Messiah. As a result, they will become "Messianic Jews," which means that they also make Him Lord of their lives.

Revelation 7 – To their dismay, the newly saved will begin to see many who have given their lives to the Lord becoming martyred for their beliefs. Delightfully, many Jewish people will now become a part of Christendom and we see in verse 4 that 144,000 become sealed. 12,000 from each tribe were standing before the throne, clad in white robes. Scripture states that the Lamb of God, Jesus, was in the <u>center</u> of that throne.

During this first quarter, the biggest evangelistic movement ever will be seen on earth, with more people coming to Christ than ever was heard of in the entire Christian dispensation. These new believers will now be realizing exactly what their loved ones tried to explain to them about the "Seven Year Tribulation" period. They will become aware that this person, who at this juncture, has called himself a peace maker, is really the antichrist who needs to be watched.

— SECOND QUARTER —
Within the Seven Year Tribulation Period

In *Revelation 8-9,* we see what is beginning to happen on earth as the seven Angels who had the "Seven Trumpets" prepared themselves to blow them (in Heaven). On earth, we see plagues, a giant burning meteorite hits the Mediterranean Sea and the water turns to blood, and another pollutes the water supply of three rivers, etc.

Revelation 10-11:14 gives a parenthetical view of the last half of the tribulation people. In the second quarter we see where God sends two witnesses to spread the Gospel of Christ. Remember, the church has been Raptured, so that means that there no longer was anyone to teach others of Christ. Remember, in the first quarter, the ones who <u>did</u>

witness were martyred and 144,000 Jewish evangelists were taken to Heaven.

Now, these two witnesses are doing what Christian believers used to do. The antichrist becomes disgruntled and has them killed at the 3½ year mark. However, after 3 days, they rise up and are taken into Heaven. This means that these evangelists are now gone no leaders to spread the Gospel of Jesus any more.

Revelation 12 gives us a view of the ENTIRE Biblical period and the tribulation period, including the time that satan was thrown down from Heaven to the earth with his angelic cohorts.

Revelation 13 gives us a more detailed description of the first quarter. We are introduced to the "Beast of the SEA" [antichrist], who is of a mixed nationality. meaning he is not a Jew. We then become aware of the "Beast of the EARTH [false Prophet], who is a Jew. The false Prophet makes the earth and those who dwell in it worship the antichrist. It is he who will be equipped by satan and the antichrist to perform miracles and supernatural signs. The false Prophet will also have power to deceive the very elect. This will be a counterfeit trinity.

- Satan counterfeits "The Father"
- The antichrist counterfeits the "Son, Jesus Christ"
- The false Prophet counterfeits the "Holy Spirit"

At the end of the 3½ year period, the antichrist will receive a wound in his head and will die. At that time the world will see him having a supernatural healing, rising up again, and duplicating Christians resurrection. At this point, the spirit of satan will have entered that being [antichrist] and all hell breaks lose from that time on. Evil will be personified as never before.

From that point in time is when the antichrist will have power to perform signs and wonders. This will be the greatest anti-Semitic movement the world has ever known. The antichrist will seek to put to death all those not bearing the mark of the beast, as well as those who will not bow down and worship him as God.

— THIRD QUARTER —
Within the Seven Year Tribulation Period

Revelation 14 begins to show us that though it could look bleak, we do have hope. We see that though satan has not stopped his quest to destroy the Christian faith, and has also pulled out all throttles as far as possible with the intent to win, God is still on the throne. In *verse 8,* it says, *"Fallen, fallen is Babylon the great, she who has made all the nations drink the wine of passion of her immorality."* This speaks of two distinct factions of Babylon....the religious Babylon and the commercial Babylon.

Revelation 16 launches the third quarter, introducing the Seven Bowls of Wrath of God onto the earth.

Revelation 17 says, *"Fallen, fallen is Babylon..."* The first 'fallen' is the "Religious Babylon" which was formulated by the antichrist to simulate the church that was taken at the Rapture. His [antichrist's] every intent is to use her [the church] until he no longer needs her, and then he will destroy her. You might equate the antichrist's usage of religious Babylon with a man who determines to pursue a young lady with the intent to conquer and use her. Once he has succeeded in raping her, he then throws her out, treating her as used trash.

In this quarter, we see God sending an "Angel" to spread the Gospel of Jesus Christ.

- In the first quarter – the <u>new believers</u> who turned to their Bibles when their Christian loved ones had disappeared, plus the <u>Jewish converts</u>, who finally realized that Jesus was indeed their Promised Messiah, were the ones who spread God's Word.
- In the second quarter, God sent <u>two witnesses</u> to spread the Gospel. They died and were left in the street for three days, allowing the world to see them via the media and TV. However, they were resurrected and then were gone.
- Now, in the third quarter, God sends an <u>Angel</u> – the first time ever – to spread the Good News of the Gospel.

— FOURTH QUARTER —
Within the Seven Year Tribulation Period

Revelation 18:21-24 – The second *fallen* was the "Commercial Babylon," which the antichrist depended upon and had every intention to protect. Instead, the tables get turned and it is now God's turn to pull out HIS throttles. The intent is to proceed to destroy the "Commercial Babylon," which ultimately will bring about the demise of satan and his works.

"Then a strong angel took up a stone like a great mill-stone and threw it into the sea, saying, "So will Babylon, the great city, be thrown down with violence, and will not be found any longer. And the sound of harpists and musicians and flute-players and trumpeters will not be heard in you any longer; and no craftsman of any craft will be found in you any longer; and the sound of a mill will not be heard in you any longer; and the light of a lamp will not shine in you any longer; and the voice of the bridegroom and bride will not be heard in you any longer; for your merchants were the great men of the earth, because all the nations were deceived

by your sorcery. And in her was found the blood of Prophets and of saints and of all who have been slain on the earth."

This great city was considered the music capital of the world. If you recall, satan was God's Number 1 worship leader before he was thrown out of Heaven. So, it is of no surprise that he would consider music of great importance.

Chapter Thirty-Three

— THE MILLENIAL REIGN IN THE NEW JERUSALEM ON EARTH —

The beginning of the Millennium – There are literally hundreds of verses in the Bible (*Daniel 2:31-45; Psalm 2; Ezekiel 36-48; Zechariah 14; Isaiah 65:20*) that predict an earthly kingdom of God, ruled by the Son of God, and superseding all the kingdoms of the world.

Revelation 19:1-4 says, "After these things I heard something like a loud voice of a great multitude in Heaven, saying, 'Hallelujah! Salvation and glory and power belong to our God; BECAUSE HIS JUDGMENTS ARE TRUE AND RIGHTEOUS; for He has judged the great harlot who was corrupting the earth with her immorality, and HE HAS AVENGED THE BLOOD OF HIS BOND-SERVANTS ON HER.' And a second time they said, 'Hallelujah! HER SMOKE RISES UP FOREVER AND EVER.' And the twenty-four elders and the four living creatures fell down and worshiped God who sits on the throne saying, 'Amen Hallelujah!' "

Never before in Scripture has the word "Hallelujah!" been used. It will not happen until Babylon is finally destroyed.

Revelation 20:1-5 says, *"Then I saw an angel coming down from heaven, holding the key of the abyss and a great chain in his hand. And he laid hold of the dragon, the serpent of old, who is the devil [satan], and bound him for a thousand years; and he threw him into the abyss, and shut it and sealed it over him, so that he would not deceive the nations any longer, until the thousand years were completed; after these things he must be released for a short time. Then I saw thrones, and they sat on them, and judgment was given to them. And I saw the souls of those who had been beheaded because of their testimony of Jesus and because of the word of God, and those who had not worshiped the beast or his image, and had not received the mark on their forehead and on their hand; and they came to life and reigned with Christ for a thousand years.*

The rest of the dead did not come to life until the thousand years were completed. This is the first resurrection."

Satan will be bound for 1000 years. All believers who died prior to the Rapture were resurrected a thousand years before this judgment (Great White Throne Judgment) and their works were judged at the "Judgment Seat of Christ." *2 Corinthians 5:10, "For we must all appear before the judgment seat of Christ, so that each one may be recompensed for his deeds in the body, according to what he has done, whether good or bad."*

We read that those who have already died in sin, as well as those who will die in sin, will not see the reign or kingdom on earth for these 1000 years. They must wait and be resurrected after the millennium, to be judged at their final judgment, called "The Great White Throne Judgment."

Revelation 20:6 – This tells us that those who were willing to die for their testimony are blessed and holy, and would not have to endure the seven year tribulation, but will come back with Christ and reign with Him during the thousand years.

In *Revelation 20:10* – The antichrist and the false Prophet are already in the "Lake of Fire." They are actually its first occupants, and according to Scripture, will remain there forever and ever. *"And the devil who deceived them was thrown into the lake of fire and brimstone, where the beast and the false Prophet are also; and they will be tormented day and night forever and ever."*

Revelation 20:11 – The Great White Throne Judgment follows the thousand year reign of Christ, and this will be the final judgment. Only the wicked dead who had remained in their graves at the time of the Rapture, and the unbelievers who came out of the millennial reign, are left to be judged. It is interesting to note that during the millennial reign all those who became unbelievers never went beyond 100 years of age. The believers remain alive throughout.

At this judgment:

- *Revelation 20:11* – Those who died never having made the choice to make Jesus the Lord of their lives, and who had remained in their graves at the time the Christians were Raptured, just prior to the Seven Year Tribulation, will be judged. There will be no hiding place for them.
- The wicked dead, the great and the small will stand before God. But the greatness of the great will be of no value. *Romans 3:12* tells us that *"there is none who does good, there is not even one."* It does not matter how noble, how moral, how upright, how devout, or how good a person lives his life, the bottom line still is that Jesus was the sacrifice that provided for us the opportunity to come back to the Father. What satan was given by Adam that brought each of us into a sin-state life, was redeemed by the suffering of Jesus. It is only HE Who has the power to bring us to the Father.

193

He DID that! Now it is up to each of us to receive Him as our Lord. This is our only guarantee.

• *Revelation 20:12* – The Book of Life will be opened. The "Book of Life" is different from the "Lambs Book of Life." God began His genealogy in His "Book of Life" from the very beginning. Moses talks about it in *Exodus 32* when he intercedes for the Israelites. The "Lamb's Book of Life" belongs to Jesus. You <u>can</u> lose out and have your name removed from the "Book of Life," whereas, once your name is in the "Lamb's Book," it will <u>never</u> be removed.

Book of Life – *Exodus 32, 33; Psalm 69:28; Daniel 12:1; Philippians 4:3*. The New Testament refers to this book eight times. Even though the Old Testament. does not call it the <u>Book of Life</u>, it mentions a book three times in which names are written. <u>The Lamb's Book of Life</u> in *Revelation 13:8* appears to contain only the names of those believers who have lived <u>since the cross</u>.

There are three reasons for having one's name blotted out of the Book of Life:

1) For sinning against God – and being unclean – *Revelation 21:27*
2) For not being clothed in the righteousness of Christ – *Revelation 3:5*
3) For taking away from the words of the book of this prophecy – *Revelation 22:18-19*

<u>Bottom line</u> – If a person's name appears in the "Lambs Book of Life," it will remain in the "Book of Life" also, which originated since the beginning of time. However, if a person's name, which is automatically entered into the "Book of Life" when that person is born, does not ever get

entered into the "Lamb's Book of Life," then that name will be removed from the "Book of Life" as well. In other words, when we die, our names are either in BOTH books or NEITHER book.

You might be wondering what happens to the Old Testament saints who died. Scripture tells us that when Jesus was resurrected from the dead, graves were opened at that time and, people saw these saints of old walking (*Matthew 27:51 "Behold, the veil of the temple was torn in two from the top to the bottom; and the earth did quake, and the rocks were split; And the graves were opened; and many bodies of the saints that slept were raised; and came out of the graves after His resurrection, and went into the holy city, and appeared unto many."*). They are with the New Testament saints now, awaiting our arrival.

The dead will be judged according to their deeds – *Revelation 20:12* states, *"And I saw the dead, the great and the small, standing before the throne, and books were opened; and another book was opened, which is the book of life; and the dead were judged from the things which were written in the books, according to their deeds."*

God is a just God, and since there are degrees of punishment in hell, some will be punished more than others. *Luke 12: 42-44, "And the Lord said, 'Who then is the faithful and sensible steward, whom his master will put in charge of his servants, to give them their rations at the proper time? Blessed is that slave whom his master finds so doing when he comes. Truly I say to you that he will put him in charge of all his possessions.'"*

- *Revelation 20:14* – There will be no acquittal, no higher court to which the lost may appeal. They are simply lost, and lost forever; damned to all eternity, and that without hope. The "Lake of Fire" is the second death.

- *Revelation 20:15* – If anyone's name is not found written in the Book of Life, then he is thrown into the "Lake of Fire." In a sense, this is God's double check at the "Great White Judgment Throne," for as a man comes forward, he will be judged by the book of the law, by the Lamb's Book of Life, and by the deeds done in the flesh taken from the books of his works. Just before he is cast into the "Lake of Fire," he is given a double check.

This double check in the Book of Life points out a consistent Scriptural principle —- that there are only two kinds of people. The Bible repeatedly refers to believing or unbelieving, saved or unsaved, condemned or not condemned, righteous or unrighteous, just or unjust, wise or unwise. Either you are "IN" or you are "OUT."

To reiterate – one does not need to have his name entered into the Book of Life, for if he is alive, it is already there; God is not willing that any should perish, but that all should come to repentance. Therefore, when someone is born – his name is automatically placed in the "Book of Life." However, in order to KEEP it there, he must also have his name written in the "Lamb's Book of Life."

Revelation 20:7 shows us that satan will be released from his prison and will set out to deceive the nations in the four corners of the earth. During the millennial reign, people will still be given a free CHOICE. Satan gets his last chance to lure anyone into his domain. You would perhaps think that there is no way anyone would choose to abolish God and get sucked in by satan. However, we need to realize that one thousand years will have gone by and time erases the excitement and even the memory of what had transpired during the millennium.

Revelation 21 introduces the eternal future planned by God, with chapters 21 and 22 providing more details of this state than any other book in the Bible.

- *A new Heaven (21:1)*
- *A new earth (21:1)*
- *A New Jerusalem (21:2)*
- *A new paradise (22:1-5)*
- *A new source of light (22:5)*
- *A new place for God's throne (22:3)*

— DIFFICULT TIMES WILL COME —

Paul tells us in *2 Timothy 3:1-5*, *"But realize this, that in the last days difficult times will come.*

For men will be lovers of self, lovers of money, boastful, arrogant, revilers, disobedient to parents, ungrateful, unholy, unloving, irreconcilable, malicious gossips, without self-control, brutal, haters of good, treacherous, reckless, conceited, lovers of pleasure rather than lovers of God, holding to a form of godliness, although they have denied its power; avoid such men as these."

Whether we want to believe it or not, perilous times WILL come. We have already seen sexual perversion exploited on prime time TV, not to mention hearing of daily rampant killings, etc. As the world falls prey to more and more violence, so also will God's people rise up and take authority. Therefore – as the sin increases, so will God's people rise to the occasion.

You could compare it to a farmer's crop, which has many thistles and weeds growing along with it. If weeds are pulled prematurely, the crop could come out with the weeds. So, in order to preserve the crop, often the farmer will wait until harvest time, separating the weeds from the crop.

This is a comparison to the difficult times we will face because just as the crop and weeds grow together so will the evil and the good rise simultaneously. Those who have no relationship with the Lord are the ones who could experience terror as the End Time approaches. But, those in Christ will know what God has promised, and will take the authority that has been given to them by Jesus Christ. They will live with the confidence and assurance of their safety and eternal salvation because of God's protection over them.

Chapter Thirty-Four

— PROPHETIC WORDS —

*D*aniel 9:25 reveals the time frame, so we would know when the Messiah will come. It is written, *"Know therefore and understand, that from the going forth of the commandment to restore and to build Jerusalem unto the Messiah, the Prince shall be seven weeks, and threescore and two weeks: the street shall be built again, and the wall, even in trouble filled times."* The commandment did come forth to restore and build Jerusalem. The street was built. The wall was rebuilt, even in trouble filled times, just as Daniel had said. The time frame Daniel gave is seven weeks, threescore and two weeks or 483 years. From this, we see that the initial coming of the "MESSIAH," the PRINCE, <u>could be expected to appear over 1900 years ago.</u>

Isaiah 49:5 further tells us, the Messiah will come when Israel is not gathered. *"And now the LORD says, who formed me from the womb to be his servant, to bring Jacob back to him, and that Israel might be gathered to him, for I am honored in the eyes of the LORD, and my God has become my strength."* Israel was under Roman rule 1950 years ago. Messiah could not initially come today to fulfill Daniel's prophecy or Isaiah's prophecy, as Israel is currently gathered as a nation. Thus, according to God's Word, the initial coming of Messiah <u>was about 2000 years ago.</u>

In *Deuteronomy 18:15, 18, 19,* Moses tells of the Messiah with these words, *"The LORD your God will raise up for you a Prophet like me from among you, from your brethren – him you shall heed. I will raise up for them a Prophet like you from among their brethren; and I will put my words in his mouth, and he shall speak to them all that I command him. And whoever will not give heed to my words which he shall speak in my name, I myself, will require it of him."* God's Word has given us the time frame that Messiah would come; also that He shall be a Prophet and shall be from the people of Israel. Then God's Word gives us a warning. If someone will not hearken unto this Man, when the Messiah comes forth, he shall perish; as it is written, *"I will require it of him."*

Isaiah 7:14 gives us additional information on the coming Messiah. *"Therefore the Lord himself will give you a sign. Behold, a young woman shall conceive and bear a son, and shall call his name Immanuel."* Thus, we now know that the Messiah shall come from the Jews, and He shall be born of a virgin. *Isaiah 49:5* further tells of the Messiah, *"And now the LORD says, who formed me from the womb to be his servant, to bring Jacob back to him, and that Israel might be gathered to him, for I am honored in the eyes of the LORD, and my God has become my strength."* Isaiah proclaims that God will form the Messiah in the womb—the womb of a virgin. The Messiah shall bring salvation to the END of the EARTH; He is the REDEEMER of ISRAEL, and is called God's Holy One. Yet, Isaiah tells us that He will be "despised and abhorred."

Daniel 9:24, "Seventy weeks (of years, or 490 years) are decreed upon your people and upon your holy city [Jerusalem], to finish and put an end to transgression, to seal up and make full the measure of sin, to purge away and make expiation and reconciliation for sin, to bring in everlasting righteousness (permanent moral and spiritual rectitude in every area and relation) to seal up vision and prophecy and Prophet, and to anoint a Holy of Holies."

Daniel 9:25, "Know therefore and understand that from the going forth of the commandment to restore and to build Jerusalem until [the coming of] the Anointed One, a Prince, shall be seven weeks [of years] and sixty-two weeks [of years]; it shall be built again with [city] square and moat, but in troublous times."

Daniel 9:26. "And after the sixty-two weeks [of years] shall the Anointed One be cut off or killed and shall have nothing [and no one] belonging to [and defending] Him. And the people of the [other] prince who will come will destroy the city and the sanctuary. Its end shall come with a flood; and even to the end there shall be war, and desolations are decreed."

Daniel 9:27, "And he [this is the Antichrist] shall enter into a strong and firm covenant with the many for one week [seven years]. And in the midst of the week he shall cause the sacrifice and offering to cease [for the remaining three and one-half years]; and upon the wing or pinnacle of abominations [shall come] one who makes desolate, until the full determined end is poured out on the desolator."[Amp]

As we study Daniel's prophecy, we note that within the seventy weeks (or seventy sets of sevens, which is 490 years) certain things were to be accomplished: *Daniel 9:24*

- To make an end of sins
- To make reconciliation for injustice
- To bring in everlasting righteousness
- To seal up the vision and prophecy
- To anoint the most holy

In other words, to summarize:

- The seven year tribulation *will* come to pass
- The antichrist *will* appear
- Jesus *will* come back with the saints of God
- The antichrist *will* meet his demise
- There *will* be a thousand year reign on earth
- There *will* be a final judgment
- Finally, all those who have accepted Jesus Christ as Lord and Savior *will* reign with Him forever and ever in the New Jerusalem, the city of God.

Chapter Thirty-Five

— A DEEPER LOOK INTO
WHAT JESUS SAYS —

John tells us in *1 John 5:10-12, "He who believes in the Son of God has the testimony in himself. He who does not believe God has made him a liar, because he has not believed in the testimony that God has borne to his Son. And this is the testimony that God gave us eternal life, and this life is in his Son. He who has the Son has life; he who has not the Son of God has not life."* This is very clear and simple! John explains that Jesus is the One Who fulfilled Plan "B" that God had to resort to and encourages us to heed it.

John also tells us in *1 John 5:20, "And we know that the Son of God has come and has given us understanding, to know him who is true; and we are in him who is true, in his Son Jesus Christ. This is the true God and eternal life."* John lets us know that God came in the form of His Son. The Holy Spirit conceived in Mary's womb the Messiah.

John 8:12 - "When Jesus spoke again to the people, he said, "I am the light of the world. Whoever follows me will never walk in darkness, but will have the light of life." We will experience a new understanding once we receive Him into our lives. Prior to receiving Jesus into our lives, we basically are clueless. Until then, the Christian message is meaningless to us. The comprehension of God's Word can be understood ONLY AFTER receiving Jesus into our lives. Then, we will see that LIGHT that He is speaking of.

John 8:51 – "Verily, verily I say unto you, if a man keep my saying he shall never see death." Yes, the body will die; this is the shell we live in. However, our spirit will live forever if we receive Jesus as our Savior. The death will be there only if we refuse to accept Him. That death referred to here means the "alienation from God forever."

John 10:9 – "I am the gate; whoever enters through me will be saved. He will come in and go out, and find pasture." What a delight it will be to come and go as you please in Heaven!

John 10:27, 28 – "My sheep hear my voice, and I know them, and they follow me: and I give unto them eternal life and they shall never perish, neither shall any man pluck them out of my hand." Again, Jesus tells us that He was sent to make sure we would have eternal life, fellowshipping with Him and the Father in Heaven.

John 14: 6 – "Jesus answered, "I am the way and the truth and the life. No one comes to the Father except through me." Jesus Himself proclaimed that He was the one God was speaking of when God spoke to satan in *Genesis 3*, explaining that Jesus will crush his head...take back God's authority, that the only thing satan could do was to bruise Jesus' heel.

Just before Jesus arose on the third day, He descended to the gates of hell, grabbed the "keys" that had originally belonged to God, and took them away from satan. At this point all authority was again back in the hands of God, the Father. Mission Accomplished!

Chapter Thirty-Six

— SOLIDIFYING OUR FUTURE —

*R*omans 3:23-24, *"...all have sinned and fallen short of the glory of God, yet they are justified by His grace as a gift, through the redemption which is in Christ Jesus."* Paul reminds us that because of Adam's sedition in the Garden – all of us were born into a sin-filled state, and as a result, were falling short of the glory of God, doomed to everlasting suffering. This gift he is speaking of is that we are able to attain glory by merely accepting Jesus as our Messiah, our Lord, and our Savior.

He was the One Who was sent to redeem us from that sin state. Acceptance of the sent Messiah enables us to be able to come to the Father. Jesus is the One Who was born of a virgin (Joseph was not His biological father). God, the Father, impregnated Mary through the Holy Spirit. That is why Jesus was considered sinless. He was both God and man, and the One Who was prophesied about by the Prophets of Old. Jesus was the very One Whom God had chosen to redeem us.

It was Jesus Who took the sin of the world onto HIS body on the Cross in order that we now can choose to have access to our Heavenly Home. This is "Why Jesus is the ONLY Way to God the Father!"

We have been given an opportunity to solidify our future. We can choose to accept Jesus as our Messiah and make Him our Lord and Savior, thereby knowing that as a result, we now can reside in Heaven forever with God the Father, His son, Jesus, and the Holy Spirit for eternity. The other choice is that we <u>not</u> do it, thereby losing out on that special commodity provided by Plan "B," which God provided for us through His Son, Jesus Christ.

Ephesians 1:3-14, "Praise be to the God and Father of our Lord Jesus Christ, who has blessed us in the Heavenly realms with every spiritual blessing in Christ. For He chose us in Him, before the creation of the world, to be holy and blameless in His sight! In love He predestined us to be adopted as His sons through Jesus Christ, in accordance with His pleasure and will – to the praise of His glorious grace, which He has freely given us in the One He loves."

"In Him we have redemption through his blood, the forgiveness of sins, in accordance with the riches of God's grace that He lavished on us with all wisdom and understanding. And He made known to us the mystery of His will according to His good pleasure, which He purposed in Christ, to be put into effect when the times will have reached their fulfillment – to bring all things in Heaven and on earth together under one head, even Christ."

"In Him we were also chosen, having been predestined according to the plan of Him who works out everything in conformity with the purpose of His will, in order that we, who were the first to hope in Christ, might be for the praise of His glory. And you also were included in Christ when you heard the word of truth, the Gospel of your salvation. Having believed, you were marked in him with a seal, the promised Holy Spirit, who is a deposit guaranteeing our inheritance

until the redemption of those who are God's possession – to the praise of his glory."

Paul reminds us of the fact that God had predestined all children of God to be adopted into His family. The thing is, it is left up to the individual whether they become a child of God. God has adopted us by Jesus Christ to Himself, to His pleasure and His will. The understanding of that *"mystery of His will that is made known to us,"* as stated in *Ephesians 1:9,* happens after we make the decision to receive Jesus as our Savior. The knowledge of the mystery has always been there, however, it takes the decision on our part to accept Jesus as our Savior to grasp it.

To reiterate, some have the wrong conception of the meaning of pre-destination. They feel that they are either predestined to go to Heaven or to hell. I would like to correct that erroneous thought. The truth is that according to *Ephesians 1*, the PLAN was predestined and foreknown, not the individual conformity to that plan.

Paul also tell us in *Romans 8:29* that *"For those God foreknew He also predestined to be conformed to the likeness of his Son, that He might be the firstborn among many brothers."* He has called all men and given them the free will to reject or accept His call. Those who accept, He has foreknown will be made righteous. Those who reject, He has foreknown and predestined that they will be consigned to eternal hell.

The word "eternity" seems foreign to us, as we cannot possibly comprehend the full meaning as God knows it. Our minds can move out to a certain depth into the future, but then there comes a point where everything becomes vague. Nevertheless, no matter how feebly we catch a glimpse of eternity, without a doubt, the wisest choice is to choose to frolic with God forever, rather than suffer with satan and his cohorts eternally.

When it comes down to it, why would anyone want more of the pain they have experienced during their earthly lifetime? Satan has done enough damage. We have a way of escape, never having to deal with him any longer. Personally, I choose the peace, love, joy, and a freedom that my God will provide. May you choose to do the same!

— WHY WE SHOULD BE OBEYING GOD NOW —

Proverbs 29:1, NIV says, "A man who remains stiff-necked after many rebukes will suddenly be destroyed – without remedy."

Some people have the mistaken idea that when the direction of the Holy Spirit comes to them, they can just ignore it for a while if they want to, and then obey Him later in their own good time. A common thought is, "I know what I am doing is wrong. I know my lifestyle is not right, but I am just going to do it a while longer. Then I will get things straightened out with the Lord."

Let me warn you, that is an extremely dangerous thing to do because God says that when you refuse His guidance your heart grows hard. It is not that God's grace does not extend to you anymore, or that He would not forgive you if you turned to Him, but SIN will callous your heart to the point where you cannot hear Him calling anymore.

That is what happened to the Children of Israel when God instructed them to go in and possess the [Promised] land, but they flatly refused. Of course, they thought they had good reasons for refusing. They were so full of fear and unbelief that they actually thought if they did what God said, they would then be destroyed. But, you know, it does not matter how good your reasons are for disobeying God, disobedience will still cost you and your heart will still be hardened.

The Children of Israel were a stiff-necked people who would not trust God; consequently He could not lead them into the Promised Land and provide for them the blessings He had planned.

If you recall, God had asked two leaders from each of the twelve tribes to scout out the Promised Land. Instead of them coming back with faith and encouragement, only TWO out of the twelve returned with a positive report. Out of the twelve, only two returned with faith and exuberance to be able to conquer their Promised Land. The rest were filled with fear and unbelief, declaring that there were giants in the land. Their fear and doubt caused them to feel like grasshoppers in the sight of their adversaries, and so they convinced everyone that no one could survive. Instead of having faith in what <u>God</u> promised them, they lived in fear and distrust, allowing the circumstances to dictate their future. As a result, they were doomed to die in the wilderness.

Their scouting time lasted forty DAYS, so God declared that everyone would stay in the wilderness one year for every day they were out. Hence, it was <u>then</u> that the "40 years of wandering" in the wilderness was established.

Numbers 19:28-38 says, "Say to them, 'As I live,' says the LORD, 'just as you have spoken in My hearing, so I will surely do to you; your corpses will fall in this wilderness, even all your numbered men, according to your complete number from twenty years old and upward, who have grumbled against Me."

"Surely you shall not come into the land in which I swore to settle you, except Caleb, the son of Jephunneh, and Joshua, the son of Nun. Your children, however, whom you said would become a prey—I will bring them in, and they will know the land which you have rejected. But as for you, your corpses will fall in this wilderness."

"Your sons shall be shepherds for forty years in the wilderness, and they will suffer for your unfaithfulness, until

your corpses lie in the wilderness. According to the number of days which you spied out the land, forty days, for every day you shall bear your guilt a year, even forty years, and you will know My opposition. I, the LORD, have spoken, surely this I will do to all this evil congregation who are gathered together against Me."

"In this wilderness they shall be destroyed, and there they will die. As for the men whom Moses sent to spy out the land and who returned and made all the congregation grumble against him by bringing out a bad report concerning the land, even those men who brought out the very bad report of the land died by a plague before the LORD."

"But Joshua the son of Nun, and Caleb, the son of Jephunneh, remained alive out of those men who went to spy out the land.'"

In other words, all of their children under 20 years of age would be allowed to enter the Promised Land with Joshua and Caleb. The rest were doomed to die in the wilderness. God would have to wait 40 years before He would lead the new generation into the Promised Land.

Imagine how this generation of grumbling, fear filled, Israelites must have felt now that they knew they were to have to remain in this dismal place, and <u>sometime</u>, between God's pronouncement, and when the new generation is privileged to enter the Promised Land, <u>they would die</u>. What a price to pay for disobedience!

Take a lesson from that and do not play around with sin. When God tells you what you need to do, do not put Him off thinking it will be easier to do it later, or not at all. That decision could be your detriment, as it will not become easier, but WILL become harder.

When the Spirit of God comes to correct you, follow His instructions and follow them quickly. Keep your heart tender. Obey the Lord!

Chapter Thirty-Seven

— IN CONCLUSION —

B y looking at each book of the Bible, we definitely can
see a pattern. From the beginning of time, throughout
the Old Testament books, we see that satan does all he can
to try to corrupt the blood line in order to keep the Promised
Messiah from coming to fruition. Once the announcement
was made in the New Testament that the Promised Messiah
was born, satan turned his quest to do all he could to keep
Jesus from paying the price for our redemption.

Once the four Gospels showed us that Jesus indeed had
fulfilled the requirement of dying on the Cross for our redemption and salvation, satan began his final strategy. From then
until now, his goal was and is to do what he must to keep
people from accepting Jesus as their Lord and Savior.

Throughout the New Testament, we see that wherever
he failed to keep believers from receiving Christ as their
Savior, his goal took a turn to either destroy these born again
Christians through martyrdom, or try to make their ministry
ineffective. From what we have seen throughout all 66 Books
of the Bible, it is obvious that satan has every intention to
continue his attempts of destroying Christendom until the

time of his own demise, which we see happening beginning with *Revelation 18.*

God went to a great amount of effort to alter what Adam destroyed. ALL mankind would have had to end up in the "Lake of Fire" that was prepared and meant only for satan and his fallen angels, were it not for God's faithfulness and willingness to provide for us a way OUT of hell and INTO God's Heavenly Home. How did He do that? He SACRIFICED His ONLY BEGOTTEN SON and had HIM killed so that THROUGH HIM we could enter the Kingdom of God.

There is only ONE way to get to HEAVEN. Each one of us has the privilege to accept or not accept Jesus – that Messiah, whom God had sent to redeem us all. This is what brings us IN! Those who never accept Jesus need to know that by doing so, they are choosing to remain on the OUTSIDE. There is only ONE way to ENTER IN – and that is THROUGH JESUS!

We could only imagine what our world would have been like had Adam and Eve fulfilled their commission to rule. Why was it that satan was able to convince them to listen to him rather than to God? The sad outcome is that they became slaves to "the god of this world," giving up the authority that God had given to them.

How do we know that satan was actually considered the god of this world? In *Luke 3:21-22,* when Jesus was baptized by John the Baptist, the Holy Spirit landed upon Him like a dove, after which he was led into the wilderness. While in the wilderness for that 40 day period, the 'tempter' came to trip Jesus up. *Luke 4:6* tells us, *"And the devil said to Him, 'I will give You all this domain and its glory; for it has been handed over to me, and I give it to whomever I wish.'"* Had it not been so, Jesus would have called him a liar. (I would highly recommend reading *"The Supernatural Ways of Royalty,"* which was co-penned by Kris Vallotton and Bill Johnson.)

So, the bottom line is that when we die...our destination – Heaven or hell – is determined by only one thing, either we accepted Jesus as our Lord and Savior or we did not. God went to a great deal of pain to win us back – all we have to do is have Jesus become our Lord and Savior, and therefore, our Redeemer – why would ANYONE want to turn their back on Him?

EPILOGUE

WOULD YOU LIKE TO HAVE THE
ASSURANCE OF REDEMPTION?

Is God touching your heart? Would you like to know that you are one who has been redeemed? Would you like to accept Jesus as your Lord and Savior, assuring your eternal salvation and redemption? If so, please say this prayer:

Dear Heavenly Father,

Forgive me for never having understood before that it was the sin of Adam, committed in the Garden of Eden that has kept me from ever being able to spend eternity in Heaven. I now know that regardless of how good a person I thought I was, I still need to accept Jesus as my Lord and Savior.

I now understand the sacrifice that was made for my redemption. I cannot imagine the pain You must have had to endure to have Your only Son, Jesus, die a cruel death on the Cross in order for the authority that had been handed over to satan be given back to You.

I would now like to accept Jesus as my Lord and Savior. It is a delight to have the assurance of knowing that I get to spend eternity in Heaven. Thank you for making that supreme sacrifice for me. Amen

WHAT HAPPENS NOW?

The Bible is God's manual, given to us for instruction on how to live a Christian life. It was never meant to just be a history book, or a book with beautiful prose and poetry, nor was it meant to just be a storybook for us to read, to name just a few. The Bible gives instruction on how to overcome the strategies of the enemy, and sights examples of blunders that were made by others in order to help us not to make those same mistakes. The Bible, as a manual, also helps us to understand the price that was paid for us in order that we may have a royal privilege to call ourselves sons and daughters of the Most High God, and joint heirs with Jesus Christ, the Messiah Who redeemed us.

Now that you have accepted Jesus Christ as your Lord and Savior, may you be so moved by what you have learned in reading this book that you will sponge up God's Word with tenacity and remain steadfast in your new found faith!

One thing I would like to leave you with, which should remain uppermost in your mind each day, is that the Word of God is to your <u>spirit</u> as bread is to your <u>body</u>. When your body feeds on physical food, it produces a physical power called strength. When your spirit feeds on the spiritual food of the Word, it produces spiritual power called faith. And just as you cannot eat one meal and then feed on the memory of it for several days, much less weeks, you cannot remember what the Word says, and determine you will still be able to stay strong in faith. You have to read it. Even if you have read it a hundred times, you need to read it again.

You can become hungry and remember how wonderful a delicious meal tastes, however, until you actually eat that food, your body will still remain hungry, and ultimately becomes weak and undernourished. Your mouth may even salivate as you think about that meal, but to rely on only the memory of it will not give you the nourishment your body needs.

Remembering the Word of God is not enough. You must continually <u>feed</u> on what it says. Get it out and read it. Go to church and hear it preached.

One day, you will read a familiar verse, a verse that you perhaps have read thousands of times before, and suddenly God will give you the greatest revelation that you have ever had. A completely fresh revelation from that old familiar verse! And it is likely to be exactly what you needed to understand, in reference to the circumstances you are experiencing at the moment.

It is most important to know that you will get continuous results if you will make it your prerogative to spend time in prayer and in the Word of God daily. Allow the Spirit to nourish you! It is imperative that you not try to live on the <u>memory</u> of your last spiritual meal. Replenish the energy of faith within you and *"<u>Feast on the Word of God every day</u>!"*

May you experience God's richest blessings as you pursue your quest to find what God says about your righteous inheritance and may you find that from this day forward you will never have to walk alone again! There is no greater Friend than Jesus. He will walk and talk with you whenever you need a friend and choose to call upon Him.

You see…He is just crazy about you!!!

BIBLIOGRAPHY – RECOMMENDED READINGS

Edwards, Gene	*100 Days in the Secret Place*	Destiny Image	2003
Kennedy, James	*The Real Meaning of the Zodiac*	Coral Ridge Min.	1989
Renner, Rick	*Sparkling Gems from the Greek*	Teach All Nations	2003
Kris Vallotton and Bill Johnson	*The Supernatural Ways of Royalty*	Destiny Image	2006
Philip D. Yancey	*Prayer, Does It Make Any Difference*	Zondervan	2006

Printed in the United States
96649LV00003B/282/A